UK Price £3.95

# AN ILLUSTRATED GUIDE TO PISTOLS AND REVOLVERS

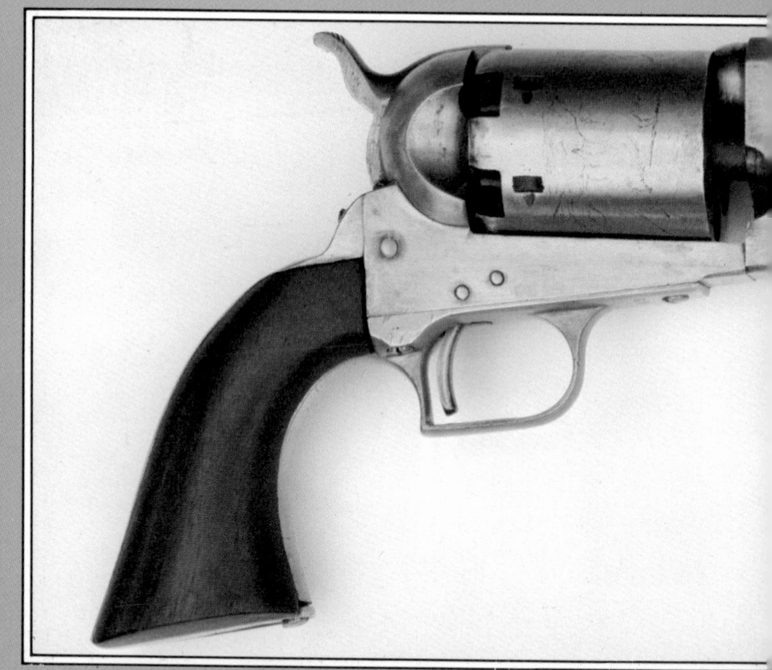

AN ILLUSTRATED GUIDE TO

# PISTOLS AND REVOLVERS

Major Frederick Myatt M.C.

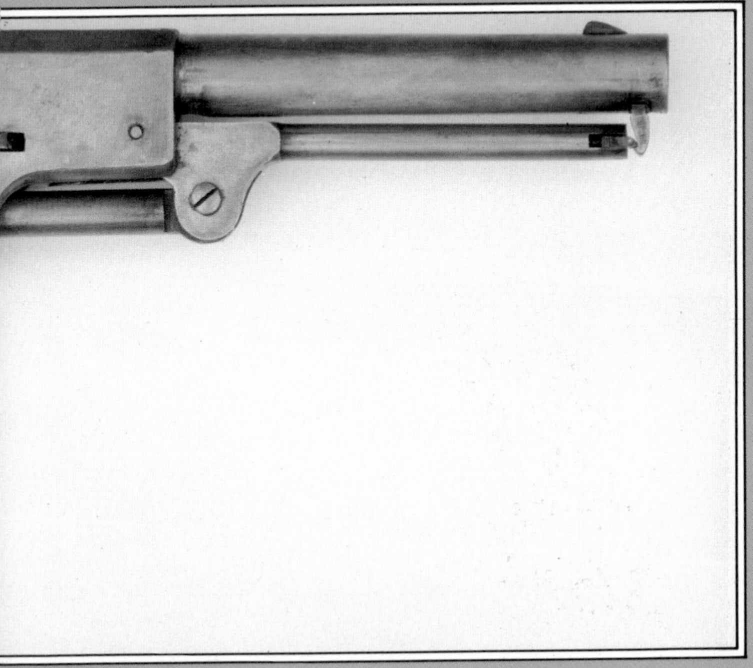

a Salamander book

Published by Salamander Books Limited
LONDON

# A Salamander Book



**ISBN 0 86101 097 3**

Distributed in the United Kingdom by New English Library Ltd.



**Publisher's note:** Some material in this book has previously appeared in *The Illustrated Encyclopedia of Pistols & Revolvers.*

# Contents

Revolvers and self-loading pistols are arranged in two groups, in approximate chronological order.

## Percussion and Cartridge Revolvers

**Author:** Major Frederick Myatt, M.C., is Curator of the Weapons Museum, School of Infantry, Warminster. Among his many books on military subjects are the Salamander titles *19th Century Firearms* and *Modern Small Arms.*

**Editor:** Richard O'Neill
**Designer:** Barry Savage
**Photography of weapons:** Bruce Scott © Salamander Books Ltd.
**Photographs:** A full list of credits is given on page 158.
**Cover illustration:** Terry Hadler
**Filmset:** Modern Text Ltd, England.
**Colour reproduction:** Tempus Litho Ltd, England.
**Printed by:** Henri Proost et Cie, Turnhout, Belgium.

# Self-Loading Pistols

# Percussion and Cartridge Revolvers

**Inset:** *A powerful cartridge makes the Magnum revolver fired by this FBI agent equally as deadly as earlier large-calibre arms.*

**Below:** *Canadian North West Mounted Police, 19th century. Man-stopping arms of Adams type were this force's hand guns.*

After the introduction of the percussion system in the earlier 19th century, the development of multi-shot pistols was relatively simple. Arms with two pairs of barrels, revolved manually through 180° to bring successive pairs of nipples under double hammers, led to arms with a cluster of four to six barrels, revolving mechanically under trigger pressure to bring each nipple in turn under a single hammer. These "pepperbox pistols" appeared by the 1830s and soon became popular. Most were small-calibre pocket models, for otherwise the barrel-cluster made them both heavy and clumsy.

The next significant development was made by the American Samuel Colt (1814-62), who envisaged a new type of revolving pistol in which the barrel-cluster of the pepperbox became a

**Above:** *Standard revolver of British officers in 1900 was the Webley Mk IV "Boer War" model.*

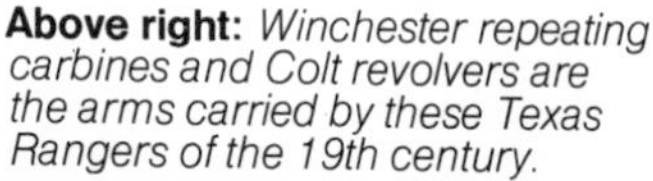

**Above right:** *Winchester repeating carbines and Colt revolvers are the arms carried by these Texas Rangers of the 19th century.*

**Right:** *A British NCO has at the ready his Enfield No 2 Mk I revolver, introduced in 1932 and in service through World War II.*

**Far right:** *Preparing for a beach landing in the Pacific, 1944, a trooper of the US 1st Cavalry uses a cleaning rod on his Smith and Wesson ·38in revolver.*

cluster of chambers brought successively into line with a single barrel. Colt never claimed to have invented the revolver principle, but to have improved it until it became viable—a step made possible by the recent perfection of the percussion cap.

There were two major requirements: the appropriate chamber must be held rigidly in line with the barrel at the moment of discharge; and partitions must be placed between the nipples so that the flash from one should not set off a chain reaction round the cylinder. By 1836 Colt had taken out patents and set up a factory at Paterson, N.J. Although his pistols were demonstrably good, there was at first little demand, but rumours of war led to increased interest by 1845—especially because Paterson revolvers had proved effective when used by mounted men in several small engagements with hostile Indians.

Colt produced a new series, concentrating on heavy-calibre models, some with detachable stocks, for use by mounted men. Although it is probable that few were ready for the Mexican War of 1846, this did not prevent their success: Colt's reputation was established and pioneers' requirements kept demand steady until the Civil War provided a final boost in 1861.

In 1851 Colt made an impressive display at the Great Exhibition, London, and soon set up a London factory. But he had a serious

British rival in Robert Adams, who entered into partnership with the Deane family and began to produce revolvers of excellent quality. Colt's arms were built up from a number of machine-made components, a method made essential by his system of mass-production by a relatively unskilled force of machine-minders supervised by a few craftsmen. This made his arms somewhat heavy. The frames and barrels of Adams' weapons were forged from single pieces of iron, giving great intrinsic strength at the added expense of employing a skilled workforce.

### The Adams Revolver in Action

Colt's locks were single-action—the hammer had to be drawn back manually for each shot—which slowed down the action but gave a lighter trigger-pull, making for accuracy. Adams' arms were self-cocking: they were fired simply by pressure on the trigger, which made the combless hammer rise and fall. This gave a heavy trigger-pull, but was a decisive factor in Britain, where most demand came from Army officers. In those days, officers often found themselves in close combat with only a light sword and a single pistol—and what they needed was speed of fire. Therefore, although Adams' pistols had only five chambers, while Colt's were "six-guns", the former rapidly outsold the latter in Britain. In 1853 the Birmingham gunsmith William Tranter did something to overcome the necessity for a heavy trigger-pull in self-cocking revolvers with his so-called double-trigger model (see pages 36-39).

### The Rammer and the Beaumont Lock

So far as British revolvers were concerned, one of the most important improvements was the general adoption of the rammer. Colt provided powerful rammers which securely seated slightly oversized bullets, kept the powder dry and virtually eliminated the risk of chain fire; but Adams initially relied on slightly oversized, tapered chambers into which bullets were forced by thumb pressure. This speeded reloading, but entailed the risk of a bullet slipping forward and preventing free rotation of the cylinder. Rammers were seen to be essential: Tranter and others patented several types, some of which were detachable.

Another development of importance was the lock invented by Lieutenant Frederick Beaumont, RE. In Beaumont's lock the arm could be fired either by simple trigger pressure or by the preliminary cocking of the hammer. Patented in 1856, this double-action lock was incorporated into Adams revolvers and soon became almost standard throughout Europe.

Once loaded, percussion revolvers were little inferior to modern arms in range, accuracy and speed of manipulation—but when the chambers had been emptied, reloading took an appreciable time. Powder and ball had to be placed into each chamber in turn and rammed home; caps had to be placed on each nipple. In combat, this was difficult for a man on foot and almost impossible for a mounted man. The calibre of percussion revolvers varied according to individual needs. Military men usually made

**Below left:** *Thomas Kavenagh of Oude, civilian winner of the Victoria Cross for gallantry during the Indian Mutiny of 1857-58, is armed with a ·44in Beaumont-Adams revolver.*

stopping power a priority, preferring an arm firing a spherical or conical bullet approaching 0·5in (12·7mm) in diameter. On a smaller scale, pocket arms of 0·32in (8mm) calibre were popular.

### The Self-Contained Cartridge

Perfection of the percussion system finally made possible the introduction of true self-contained cartridges—containing primer, propellant and projectile in a single case—which could be loaded into and fired from breechloading arms without preliminary opening or tearing of the container. As early as 1812, a Swiss named Jean Samuel Pauly invented a cartridge with a cardboard body and a brass base incorporating a cap. The next steps, in a sense divergences from the right line, were taken with the pinfire cartridge (see pages 40-43) of the 1840s and the "Volcanic" hollow bullet, containing its own propellant and percussion cap.

In 1857 Smith and Wesson acquired the patent for a bored-through revolver to fire metallic cartridges. The cases were made of copper, with percussion powder packed round the inside of the rim, to be detonated by the hammer; hence the name of "rimfire". Such revolvers were popular, although the soft copper bases of the cartridges tended to bulge backwards under the force of the exploding powder and prevent free rotation of the cylinder. Thus, copper rimfire cartridges gave place to brass cases with a central copper cap in the base. These were sufficiently robust to prevent backward bulging, while the greater elasticity of brass allowed it to expand freely under the pressure of gases, so as to give a perfect gas seal, and then to contract immediately, so as to allow for easy extraction of the case.

### Hinged Frames and Extractor Mechanisms

When Smith and Wesson's patent expired, many other firms—most notably Colt—began to make similar revolvers. Most had

**Above:** *A corporal of the US 23rd Infantry Regiment loads his ·44in Smith and Wesson Model No 3 revolver; Korea, 1951.*

**Left:** *Testing a bullet-proof vest, Washington, DC, 1923. The policeman's arm is apparently a Colt Official Police model.*

solid frames of the type developed by Adams and incorporated a loading gate as part of the standing breech, along with some kind of sliding rod under the barrel with which to knock out empty cases one by one. In 1870 Smith and Wesson produced a new type of revolver in which the frame hinged at the bottom, so that when it was opened the barrel tilted downward, rather than upward as in the firm's earlier arms. It incorporated a star-shaped extractor in the base of the cylinder, so that all the cases were ejected simultaneously when the revolver was opened. In 1877 the British firm of Webley produced a broadly similar hinged-frame revolver; thereafter, most British revolvers were made to that hinged-frame pattern.

In the United States, the enormous home market remained under the domination of Colt, particularly for large-calibre holster pistols. The Colt's disadvantage was its relatively slow system of ejecting empty cases one by one with a rod—and in 1887 this was remedied by providing a cylinder on a separate hinged crane, which could be swung out sideways so that cases were ejected simultaneously by means of a star extractor worked manually by a rod.

### The Modern Revolver

The development of the revolver was virtually complete by the end of the 19th century: since then, improvements have been largely concerned with the use of lightweight metals and new and more powerful cartridges, such as the Magnum. There became established four basic calibres: ·22in (5·6mm); ·32in (8·1mm); ·38in (9·6mm); and a larger, less clearly defined one covering

**Above:** *The revolver as image-builder: flamboyant US General George S. Patton habitually wore "six-guns" with ivory grips.*

**Left:** *Private George Stone of the Royal Sussex Regiment holds a Webley and Scott Mark VI revolver; India, 1933.*

**Right:** *A US military policeman test fires a ·38in Smith and Wesson civilian revolver into a bullet recovery tube.*

·44in (11·17mm); ·442in (11·22mm); ·45in (11·43mm); ·455in (11·55mm) and ·476in (12·1mm). There was considerable variation in the size of the propellant charge, affecting the length of the cartridge case. Broadly, in the United States the preference has been for a large charge to give good accuracy at long ranges; whereas in Europe a man-stopping bullet propelled by a quite moderate charge of powder has been the norm. These divergences have naturally led to fairly considerable differences in the length of revolver cylinders.

Revolvers provided with detachable, rifle-type butts, designed to convert them into carbines for greater accuracy at longer ranges, were also made, mainly in the United States of America, but never found wide acceptance. Such a weapon offered some advantages to a mounted man shooting from the saddle, but excellent purpose-designed carbines were so readily available for such use that most people preferred to carry two separate types of arm—although very often both fired the same cartridge, as was indeed desirable.

The future of the revolver seems to lie largely in its use by security forces. Although perhaps somewhat "old fashioned" in comparison to the self-loading pistol, it is holding its own and may even be gaining ground. It has the advantage of simplicity: it may be carried safely while fully loaded and yet be ready for immediate use by simply pulling the trigger; it is less susceptible to dirt and dust than the self-loader; and in the event of a misfire the next round comes under the hammer without delay. Its chief disadvantage is its bulky cylinder, which makes it difficult to carry concealed and which limits its capacity to no more than six rounds.

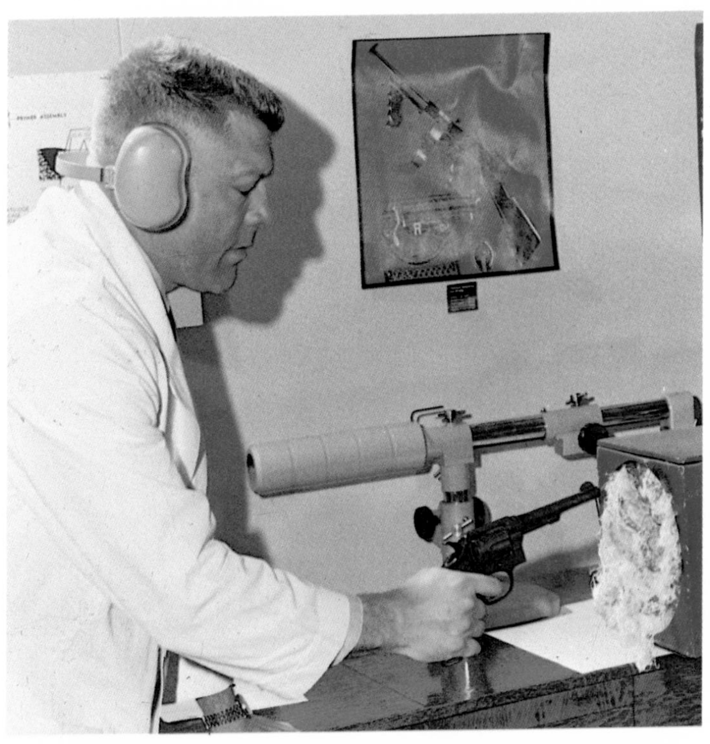

Great Britain
## COOPER PEPPERBOX PISTOL

| | |
|---|---|
| **Length:** | 7·75" (197mm) |
| **Weight:** | 17oz (·48kg) |
| **Barrel:** | 2·5" (63mm) |
| **Calibre:** | ·400" (10·2mm) |
| **Rifling:** | Nil |
| **Capacity:** | Six |
| **Muz Vel:** | c400 f/s (122 m/s) |
| **Sights:** | Nil |

United States of America
## ALLEN AND THURBER PEPPERBOX

| | |
|---|---|
| **Length:** | 7·5" (190mm) |
| **Weight:** | 23oz (·65kg) |
| **Barrel:** | 3" (76mm) |
| **Calibre:** | ·31" (8mm) |
| **Rifling:** | Nil |
| **Capacity:** | Six |
| **Muz Vel:** | c400 f/s (122 m/s) |
| **Sights:** | Nil |

Great Britain
**COOPER PEPPERBOX PISTOL**
The butt of this pistol is of chequered walnut and its top tang bears the inscription "SELF-ACTING CENTRAL FIRE REVOLVING PISTOL". Such arms made their appearance in the 1830s and were largely superseded by true revolvers within two or three decades.

United States of America
**ALLEN AND THURBER PEPPERBOX**
Ethan Allen, who set up in business as a gunmaker with his brother-in-law in the 1830s, was best known for the production of pepperbox pistols like this one: neat, compact, and of the quality traditionally associated with the firm of Allen and Thurber.

Belgium
**MARIETTE PEPPERBOX**

| | |
|---|---|
| **Length:** | 7·25" (184mm) |
| **Weight:** | 24oz (·68kg) |
| **Barrel:** | 2·8" (71mm) |
| **Calibre:** | ·38" (9·6mm) |
| **Rifling:** | Nil |
| **Capacity:** | Six |
| **Muz Vel:** | c500 f/s (152 m/s) |
| **Sights:** | Nil |

Great Britain
**TURNER PEPPERBOX**

| | |
|---|---|
| **Length:** | 9·25" (235mm) |
| **Weight:** | 32oz (·91kg) |
| **Barrel:** | 3·5" (89mm) |
| **Calibre:** | ·476" (12·1mm) |
| **Rifling:** | Nil |
| **Capacity:** | Six |
| **Muz Vel:** | c500 f/s (152 m/s) |
| **Sights:** | Nil |

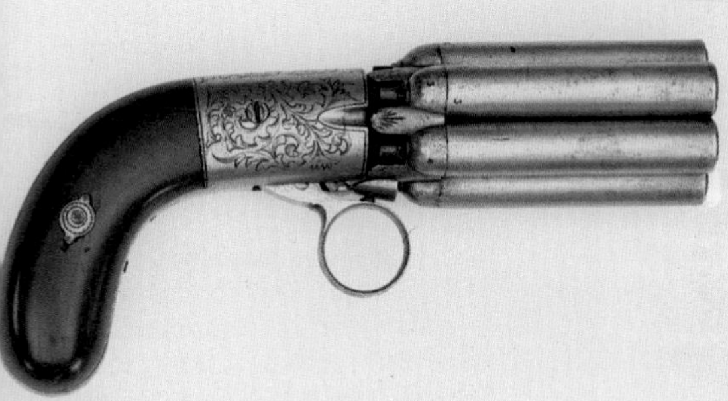

Belgium
**MARIETTE PEPPERBOX**
Pepperbox pistols, which were fast and formidable weapons in a close-quarter brawl, were most popular with civilian users. Some were made for military use: these are usually of large calibre and, if for naval service, often are fitted with belt hooks.

Great Britain
**TURNER PEPPERBOX**
This unusually large pepperbox—an arm of good quality from a well-known British provincial gunmaker of the 19th century—was possibly intended as a naval boarding pistol. Its chequered walnut butt incorporates a spring-lidded cap compartment.

Great Britain

## COOPER PEPPERBOX PISTOL

The British gunsmith J.R. Cooper produced a large number of pepperbox pistols in the period 1840-50, many based on an arm of similar type patented in Belgium in 1837 and made thereafter both there and in France, under the name of Mariette. This example, however, is of more distinctly British type. The top tang of the frame bears the inscription "J R COOPER, PATENTEE", although it is not known if it was, in fact, ever patented in England. The weapon is well, if plainly, made: its six barrels have been bored out of a solid block of metal and the grooves between the barrels bear Birmingham proof marks. The firing mechanism is internal and is of double-action only; thus, considerable pressure must be exerted on the trigger to fire. The barrels may be loaded while attached to the weapon (a separate ram-rod being provided in the case, which is not shown here), but in order to cap the nipples it is necessary to unscrew the front cap and remove the cylinder from the pistol. The nipples, which are placed in a line with the axis of the barrels, are set in deep, circular recesses, in order to reduce the risk of a multiple discharge; the slots visible at the breech end of the barrels are mainly to allow for the escape of gases. As the striker comes forward to fire the top barrel, a cylinder-stop also emerges from the bottom of the standing breech and engages in the lowest slot, thus preventing any rotation of the cylinder at the moment of firing the pistol.

United States of America

## ALLEN AND THURBER PEPPERBOX

This pistol was made in Worcester, Mass. Its six barrels are bored out of a single block of steel, with ribs between: two of the ribs bear the inscriptions "PATENTED 1837, CAST STEEL" and "ALLEN & THURBER WORCESTER". The subject of the patent referred to was, in fact, the double-action bar hammer mechanism. Steady pressure on the trigger causes the rear-hinged hammer (which is inscribed "ALLEN PATENT") to rise until the lifter hook disengages, allowing it to fall and strike the cap. The action of the trigger also rotates the barrel cluster by means of a pawl and ratchet. Access to the lock mechanism is gained by removing a plate on the left-hand side of the breech. The nipples, which are set at right-angles to the barrels, are covered by a close-fitting shield; an aperture to the right of the hammer nose gives access to them for recapping. Light pressure on the trigger lifts the nose clear of the nipple and allows the barrels to be rotated clockwise for recapping. The butt consists of a continuous metal strap made integrally with the body; both of its two wooden side plates, held by a screw, bear small, oval, escutcheon plates. The body of the weapon is ornamented with rather crude engraving, but the arm is otherwise strictly utilitarian. Although the combination of heavy trigger and obscured sight-line reduced the accuracy of arms of this type, they were nevertheless widely carried as pocket pistols in the United States and continued in production until about 1871.

Belgium
## MARIETTE PEPPERBOX

This is an example of the Mariette-type pistol, made to a design patented in Belgium in 1837 and manufactured widely thereafter in both that country and in France. This specimen is of Belgian manufacture and bears the Liège proofmarks. It is of the orthodox design of the type, in that its barrels, instead of being bored from a single block, are screwed separately on to six chambers, into which the nipples are fixed. Each barrel has four rectangular slots at 90-degree intervals round the muzzle, to facilitate its removal with a special key, and each barrel is also numbered, as is each chamber. The cluster of barrels is screwed to a spindle on the standing breech, access to which is gained by way of the central space left in the cluster of barrels. As may be seen, the nipples are in the same axis as the barrels; this reduced the chances of a misfire and made the arm neat and compact. Pressure on the ring-trigger causes the barrels to rotate, bringing each in turn into line, and also draws back and releases the internal hammer, which strikes the nipple on the lowest barrel. There are partitions between the nipples, and in addition a further shield (visible in the photograph) rises as the hammer falls to guard completely the nipple being fired. Re-capping is achieved by pressing the trigger sufficiently to allow the barrels to be manually rotated: a small slot is exposed in the right-hand side of the frame, allowing the caps to be slid into place. The butt is of ebonised plates, on a strap inscribed "MARIETTE BREVETTE".

Great Britain
## TURNER PEPPERBOX

This well-made pistol produced by Thomas Turner of Reading has six smooth-bored barrels which are drilled from a single block of steel in the usual manner; but somewhat unusually, each is numbered at the breech end, the ribs between them being stamped alternately with either a view mark or a proof mark. The nipples are at right angles to the axis of the barrels and, as may be seen, there are no partitions between them. This must have increased the risk of the barrels chain-firing. The breech also incorporates a nipple shield to prevent the percussion caps from being brushed or shaken off; however, by canalizing the flash from the cap, this must also have contributed to the risk of more than one barrel firing from a single cap. The bar hammer is of standard double-action type and requires considerable pressure on the trigger to operate it. The trigger action also activates a pawl and ratchet to rotate the barrels. These rotate on an axis pin screwed into the standing breech; they are held in place on the pin by an engraved, brass-headed screw which fits flush with the muzzles. Access to the nipples is gained through an aperture in the flash shield just to the right of the hammer, and slight pressure on the trigger raises the hammer nose from the nipples sufficiently to rotate the barrels manually in anti-clockwise direction. Unusually, this weapon is fitted with a sliding safety catch (visible behind the hammer). When this is drawn back, it locks the hammer in the down position.

Great Britain
**TRANSITIONAL REVOLVERS**

It was formerly believed that arms of this type—of which many examples are still extant—represented the "transition", from the 1830s onward, between the pepperbox pistol and the more sophisticated percussion arms of the mid-century. However, it is now thought that most date from the early 1850s, and that they in fact represent little more than cheaper substitutes for the arms of Colt, Adams and other well-known makers.

Great Britain
**TRANSITIONAL REVOLVERS**

| | |
|---|---|
| **Length:** | 11·5" (292mm) |
| **Weight:** | 35oz (·99kg) |
| **Barrel:** | 5·6" (142mm) |
| **Calibre:** | ·44" (11·2mm) |
| **Rifling:** | 14 groove, r/hand |
| **Capacity:** | Six |
| **Muz Vel:** | c500 f/s (152 m/s) |
| **Sights:** | Fixed |

Great Britain
**TRANSITIONAL REVOLVERS WITH BAYONETS**

| | |
|---|---|
| **Length:** | 12" (305mm) |
| **Weight:** | 32oz (·91kg) |
| **Barrel:** | 5·8" (147mm) |
| **Calibre:** | ·42" (10·7mm) |
| **Rifling:** | 9 groove, r/hand |
| **Capacity:** | Six |
| **Muz Vel:** | c500 f/s (152 m/s) |
| **Sights:** | Fixed |

In order to fix the folding bayonet, the stud near the muzzle is pressed: a helical spring then flicks the blade into position.

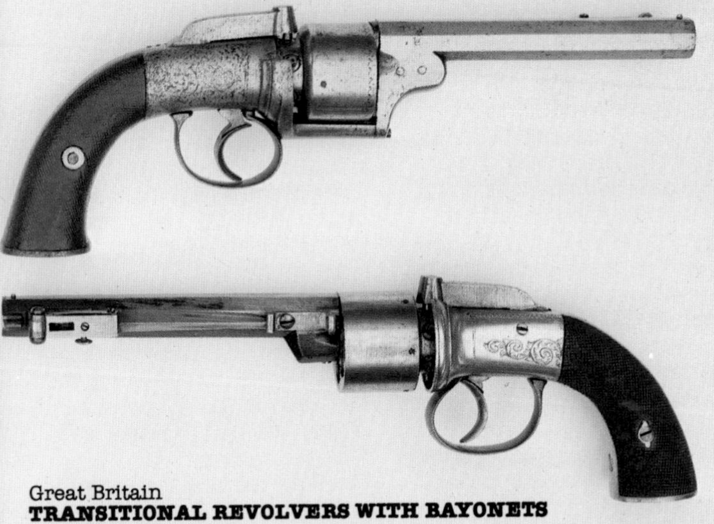

Great Britain
**TRANSITIONAL REVOLVERS WITH BAYONETS**
Although not much larger than the blade of a pen-knife, the folding bayonet could inflict a serious or even mortal wound.

Great Britain

## TRANSITIONAL REVOLVERS

There exists some element of doubt concerning the earliest date at which arms of the so-called "transitional" type were made. Colt's new revolvers must have been known to gunsmiths, if not to the general public, by the mid-1840s, and it is possible that a few so-called transitional arms were manufactured at that time, using components made for pepperbox pistols. It is probable, however, that most were made in the early 1850s, after the percussion revolver had become generally known. The revolvers shown here were made by T.K. Baker of London and are close to being a pair, although, as may be seen, the upper one has been cleaned bright at some time, while the lower arm retains most of its original blue. A somewhat old-fashioned look is given to the rifled barrels by the fact that they are octagonal for just over half their length. The cylinders are deeply rebated at the rear to give a seating for the nipples which, in orthodox pepperbox fashion, have no partitions between them; a factor increasing the risk of a chain-fire discharge. The rear faces of the cylinders are cut to form a ratchet, with a further, outer row of six slots for the cylinder stops. On each weapon, the hammer, although similar in some respects to the bar-type hammers encountered on some of the earlier pepperbox pistols, is in fact of single-action type and must be cocked for each shot; hence the provision of the long hammer spur. The action of placing the hammer at half-cock causes the cylinder to make a very slight rotation in an anti-clockwise direction; pulling the hammer back to full cock brings the next chamber into line and also locks the cylinder in such a position that the top chamber is in line with the barrel. Although positioned so as to strike centrally on top of the frame, the hammer is slightly angled, so that when the arm is cocked the foresight can be aligned with a shallow V backsight on the hammer itself. The frames of these revolvers are of German silver and incorporate nipple shields; the butt-plates, which are held by a single screw, are of walnut. Arms of this type had three basic weaknesses as compared with the later percussion revolvers: the nipples are placed at right-angles instead of straight into the charge, which increased the chance of misfires; there are no shields between the nipples; and the method by which the barrel is held in place, screwed to the axis pin without any secondary brace to the frame, is unsatisfactory. In the latter case, although the pin is robust and is firmly seated at the breech end there must be a tendency for the barrel to work loose, which would lead to loss of power, to inaccuracy and, possibly, to real danger to the firer if the chamber and barrel are actually out of alignment at the moment of firing. The arms' far from robust qualities probably led to their rejection for service use: most officers preferred to retain their comparatively old-fashioned double-barrelled pieces—or purchase one of the new revolvers produced by Colt or Adams. (The latter were both widely used in the Crimean War and the Indian Mutiny.) Revolvers of the kind seen here were, however, probably quite adequate self-defence weapons for householders and travellers.

Great Britain

## TRANSITIONAL REVOLVERS WITH BAYONETS

These two interesting arms show the lines along which the transitional revolver developed in the mid-19th century. The lower arm is almost certainly of slightly earlier date, and a reference back to the pepper-box pistols will show the influence which those earlier arms had on later developments. The lower revolver here has an octagonal, blued barrel and the top flat bears the inscription "IMPROVED REVOLVER". The cylinder is of orthodox type and, from its general appearance, could well be a cut-down cluster of pepperbox barrels (although it is not suggested that this is the case). The nipples are at right-angles to the axis of their chambers and there are no partitions. The cylinder bears Birmingham proof marks, which at least indicates its origins. The lock is of double-action type with bar hammer and orthodox trigger; as is the case with most arms of its kind, considerable pressure is required to operate the trigger. The frame, including the shield, is of German silver, quite nicely engraved; the butt, with side plates of some hard, black composition, is well-shaped but somewhat too small for a normal hand. The weapon is fitted with a folding bayonet. A well-made and well-finished weapon, it suffers from the usual defects of its type: notably the angle of the nipples and the lack of partitions between them; and, perhaps, more importantly, the fact that the barrel is attached only to the axis pin, without any additional bracing. It has the further defect that the rising hammer completely obscures the line of sight. The upper revolver also has a folding bayonet, part of which is just visible above the barrel. It will, however, be seen that there is a strong projection below the cylinder to which a corresponding projection below the barrel is firmly screwed, thus making a very considerable contribution to the strength and rigidity of the weapon. The frame of this revolver is made of iron and the butt is of a more handy size than that of the lower arm; thus, all in all, it constitutes in most respects a more robust and more serviceable arm. Data refer to the upper weapon of the two. It is 0·75in (19mm) longer in the barrel than the lower example, but otherwise of similar dimensions.

*Crimea, 1854. Transitional revolvers generally were not robust enough for service use.*

Prussia
**KUFAHL'S NEEDLE-FIRE REVOLVER**

| | |
|---|---|
| **Length:** | 9·6" (244mm) |
| **Weight:** | 22oz (·62kg) |
| **Barrel:** | 3·2" (81mm) |
| **Calibre:** | ·300" (7·62mm) |
| **Rifling:** | 5 groove, l/hand |
| **Capacity:** | Six |
| **Muz Vel:** | c500 f/s (152 m/s) |
| **Sights:** | Fixed |

Prussia
**KUFAHL'S NEEDLE-FIRE REVOLVER**
This revolver works on very similar principles to those of the famous Prussian "needle-gun" invented by von Dreyse.

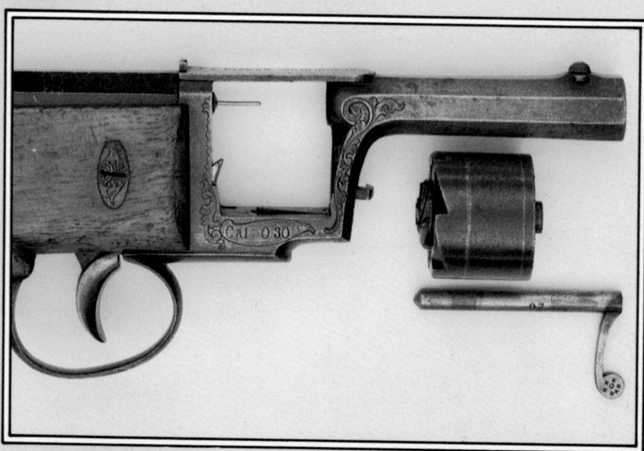

The needle-fire revolver with the cylinder and axis pin removed. The pawl which engages the ratchet at the rear of the cylinder, causing the whole to rotate, is seen protruding from the face of the standing breech. The needle is in the forward position.

United States of America
**TAPE-PRIMER REVOLVER**

| | |
|---|---|
| **Length:** | 10·5" (267mm) |
| **Weight:** | 24oz (·68kg) |
| **Barrel:** | 6" (152mm) |
| **Calibre:** | ·32" (8·1mm) |
| **Rifling:** | 7 groove, l/hand |
| **Capacity:** | Six |
| **Muz Vel:** | c550 f/s (168 m/s) |
| **Sights:** | Fixed |

United States of America
**TAPE-PRIMER REVOLVER**

| | |
|---|---|
| **Length:** | 6·6" (168mm) |
| **Weight:** | 10oz (·28kg) |
| **Barrel:** | 3" (76mm) |
| **Calibre:** | ·28" (7·1mm) |
| **Rifling:** | 7 groove, l/hand |
| **Capacity:** | Six |
| **Muz Vel:** | c500 f/s (152 m/s) |
| **Sights:** | Fixed |

United States of America
**TAPE-PRIMER REVOLVER**
The invention of the tape-primer system, which was widely used on rifles and carbines from around 1850 until after the US Civil War, is credited to Edward Maynard, a dentist, of Washington, DC.

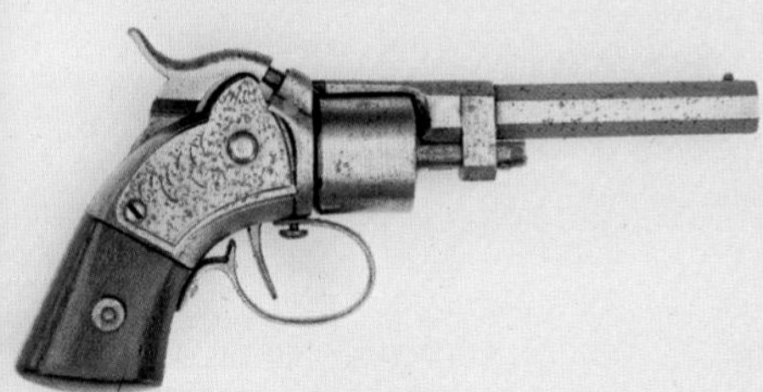

United States of America
**TAPE-PRIMER REVOLVER**
Revolvers of this type, incorporating Maynard's tape-primer, were produced by the Massachusetts Arms Company during the 1850s. The cylinder, rotated by a system of bevel gears rather than a pawl and ratchet, was the invention of Edwin Wesson (brother of the more famous Daniel B. Wesson of the Smith & Wesson partnership). A legal decision that it infringed Samuel Colt's patent forced a suspension of manufacture between 1853 and 1857.

Prussia

## KUFAHL'S NEEDLE-FIRE REVOLVER

A needle-fire weapon is one firing a consumable cartridge in which the cap is immediately behind the bullet; this necessitates a long, needle-like striker which will pierce the base of the cartridge and then pass through the powder charge in order to reach the cap. The earliest of these weapons, a breech-loading rifle, was developed by Johann Nikolaus von Dreyse as early as 1838. It was in many ways an inefficient weapon, but the mere fact that it was a breech-loader, however defective, made it a great asset to Prussia, which was soon to become a major power in Europe. In 1852, G. L. Kufahl patented in Britain a revolver which worked on very similar principles, but no British maker seemed to be at all interested in it. Kufahl therefore offered it to Franz von Dreyse, son of the inventor of the original needle-gun, who accepted the revolver and put it into production, probably in about 1854, and apparently continued to make it until 1880, long after the development and general introduction of efficient centre-fire metallic cartridges. Kufahl's revolver is also believed to have been made elsewhere on the continent. The specimen seen here has a barrel and frame made out of a single piece of iron, although the top strap, across the cylinder, has been welded on separately. The octagonal barrel is rifled and has a noticeably swamped muzzle. It is fitted with a laterally adjustable foresight; the backsight consists of a V-notch in the raised part at the rear of the top strap. The butt is a single piece of wood, partially chequered, and is held in place by a screw through the lower tang. The rear trigger-guard is also hooked into this tang, with its front end held in place by a screw. The cylinder is not bored through; instead, there is a small hole at the rear of each chamber to allow the needle to reach the front-loaded consumable cartridge. The cylinder axis pin can be removed by turning it through 90° and drawing it out from the front; a small spring stud on the left side of the frame holds it in place to avoid this process being carried out accidentally. Steady pressure on the trigger first forces the bolt forward and rotates and locks the cylinder; then it allows the needle-holder and needle to go forward and fire the cartridge. Once the trigger is released, the needle and holder are automatically retracted, thus allowing the cylinder to rotate in readiness for the next shot. The pistol, which is well made and finished, bears the inscription "Fv. V. Dreyse Sommerda" on the top strap. It is numbered "12620" on the left side of the frame; the right side bears the inscription "Cal 0·30" (visible in the photograph), which suggests that this arm was made for the British or American market. An interesting feature of this pistol – although, in view of its date, coincidental – is that it resembles some later revolvers, made specifically to fire self-contained cartridges, at the time when the Rollin – White patent for revolvers with bored-through cylinders was held by the firm of Smith and Wesson. The patent did not expire until 1869. After that date the field was wide open to any maker, and metallic cartridge revolvers appeared in great numbers from makers in all the major arms-producing countries.

United States of America
## TAPE-PRIMER REVOLVER

In 1851, Colt sued the Massachusetts Arms Company for producing revolvers with mechanically-rotated cylinders in contravention of a patent he had taken out earlier. The weapon illustrated is one of the modified versions of these. Its barrel, which is rifled, is attached to the top of the standing breech by a hinged strap which permits it to be raised to an angle of about 45° in order to remove the cylinder. The latter is mounted on a stout axis pin which protrudes slightly more than 1in (25·4mm) beyond the front face of the cylinder; the object of this extension is to provide a firm locking point for a hook which pivots round the breech end of the barrel. There is a small retaining spring on the end of the axis pin to prevent it being released accidentally. The lock is fitted with a tape-primer, which makes possible the use of a single nipple only: the flash is transmitted to the charge by means of a small hole at the rear of each chamber. When the cylinder stop pin is pushed, the cylinder may be rotated manually.

*The tape primer roll fits into the circular depression and its end is fed over the toothed wheel.*

United States of America
## TAPE-PRIMER REVOLVER

The popularity of Colt's percussion revolvers naturally led to attempts by many manufacturers to circumvent Colt's patents. In 1851, Colt sued the Massachusetts Arms Company of Chicopee Falls for contravention of his patent in respect of a mechanically-revolving cylinder. The Massachusetts Arms Company pleaded that the revolver in question, originally designed by Wesson and Leavitt, made use of a system of bevel gears rather than a pawl and ratchet to rotate the cylinder, and that it was, therefore, not bound by the patent referred to. However, the court found against the Company, which had to cease the manufacture of these particular arms until Colt's patent expired in 1857. The small pocket revolver seen here is one of the pistols modified so as not to contravene the patent. It has several interesting features. The rear end of the top strap, which is integral with the barrel, is hinged to the standing breech in such a way that it can be turned upwards through about 45°, thus allowing the cylinder to be removed by pulling it forward off its axis pin. The length of this is such that, when the cylinder is fully home, about 1in (25·4mm) protrudes beyond its front face; this extension serves as a peg on which is fixed a hook attached to the breech end of the barrel by means of a collar. The hook is held in place by a small press-stud (just visible in front of it, on the lower side of the axis pin). A single nipple is screwed into the top of the breech at such an angle that it is exactly aligned with the vent leading into the rear of each chamber.

United States of America
**COLT DRAGOON MODEL 1849**

| | |
|---|---|
| **Length:** | 13·5" (343mm) |
| **Weight:** | 68oz (1·93kg) |
| **Barrel:** | 7·5" (190mm) |
| **Calibre:** | ·44" (11·2mm) |
| **Rifling:** | 7 groove, l/hand |
| **Capacity:** | Six |
| **Muz Vel:** | c850 f/s (259 m/s) |
| **Sights:** | Fixed |

United States of America
**COLT NAVY REVOLVER**

| | |
|---|---|
| **Length:** | 12·9" (328mm) |
| **Weight:** | 39oz (1·1kg) |
| **Barrel:** | 7·5" (190mm) |
| **Calibre:** | ·36" (9·1mm) |
| **Rifling:** | 7 groove, r/hand |
| **Capacity:** | Six |
| **Muz Vel:** | c700 f/s (213 m/s) |
| **Sights:** | Fixed |

United States of America
**COLT DRAGOON MODEL 1849**
This massive revolver got its name from its primary function as a cavalry weapon—its size and weight certainly make it an unsuitable arm for a foot soldier or a civilian user.

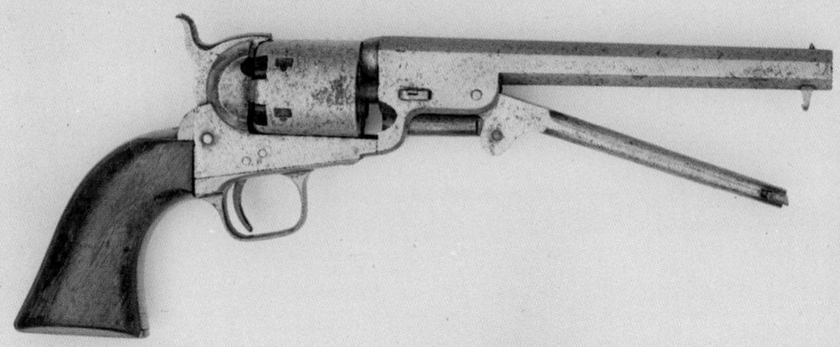

United States of America
**COLT NAVY REVOLVER**
Colt Navy revolvers lost their early popularity among British Army officers when it was found that they lacked stopping power against the powerfully-built enemies encountered in colonial warfare.

United States of America
**REMINGTON ARMY MODEL 1863**

| | |
|---|---|
| **Length:** | 13·75" (349mm) |
| **Weight:** | 44oz (1·25kg) |
| **Barrel:** | 8" (203mm) |
| **Calibre:** | ·44" (11·2mm) |
| **Rifling:** | 5 groove, r/hand |
| **Capacity:** | Six |
| **Muz Vel:** | c700 f/s (213 m/s) |
| **Sights:** | Fixed |

United States of America
**STARR REVOLVER**

| | |
|---|---|
| **Length:** | 13·5" (343mm) |
| **Weight:** | 48oz (1·36kg) |
| **Barrel:** | 7·8" (198mm) |
| **Calibre:** | ·44" (11·2mm) |
| **Rifling:** | 6 groove, l/hand |
| **Capacity:** | Six |
| **Muz Vel:** | c700 f/s (213 m/s) |
| **Sights:** | Fixed |

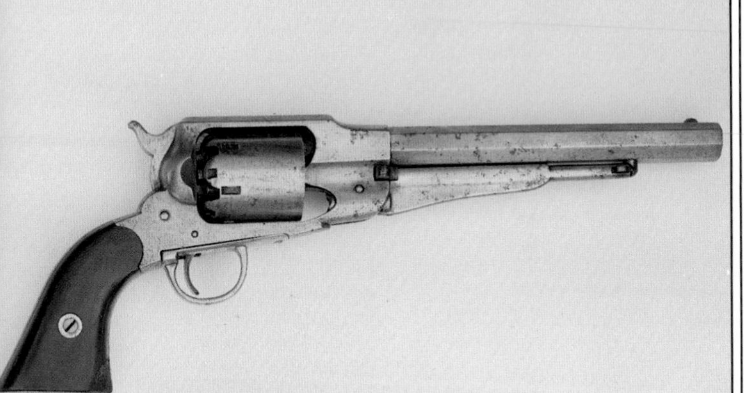

United States of America
**REMINGTON ARMY MODEL 1863**
Although the company founded in 1816 by Eliphalet Remington is now most famous for the production of long arms, it was in the later 19th century second only to Colt as a manufacturer of hand guns.

United States of America
**STARR REVOLVER**
Although this is in every respect a robust and well-made revolver, fierce competition from other makers forced the Starr Arms Company out of business in 1867, after only eleven years of production.

United States of America
## COLT DRAGOON MODEL 1849

The earliest versions of the unusually heavy arm seen here were the Walker or Witney-ville-Walker models, which appeared as a result of the increased demand for arms caused by the Mexican War of 1846. These were followed by the Dragoon series, so called because the weapons were primarily used to arm cavalry of that description. This particular specimen is the Colt Dragoon, Model 1849 (although it should be noted that it has the square-backed trigger-guard not often found at such a late date). It has a round barrel with a foresight; the backsight is incorporated into the top of the hammer. The barrel is keyed to the very robust axis pin and is further supported by a solid lug butted to the lower frame. Below the barrel is the arm's very powerful compound rammer, which forced the bullets into the chambers so tightly that neither damp nor the flash from previous shots could enter. This weapon has been over-cleaned, but traces of the engraving showing a Red Indian combat scene remain on the cylinder.

*A Canadian settler armed with a percussion revolver defends his family against hostile Indians.*

United States of America
## COLT NAVY REVOLVER

The Colt Dragoon revolver was a very powerful arm, but its method of construction meant that it had to be a massive weapon, of dimensions and weight which made it unsuitable as an arm for a man on foot or for a civilian. The next size was the Navy revolver, first introduced in 1851, which was in every respect a more manageable arm than the Dragoon and which very soon became extremely popular. Colt, having begun production at his new factory, decided that the time had come to aim at exporting on a large scale. The Great Exhibition held in London in 1851 provided him with an excellent opportunity for publicity, and his very impressive display of revolvers there attracted a great deal of attention. The revolver was then little known in England, but its merits were quickly appreciated – and Colt was ready to set up production in London almost immediately. The Colt revolver illustrated is of broadly similar type to the Dragoon, although, of course, smaller. It has an octagonal barrel with a bead foresight; the barrel is secured to the frame by means of a wedge through the very stout cylinder axis pin and is firmly braced against the lower frame. The six-chambered cylinder is plain, except for rectangular depressions for the stop, and still bears traces of engraving showing a naval engagement. The revolver has a hemispherical standing breech, in which a depression is located on the right-hand side so as to allow access to the nipples. The revolver was made in Colt's London factory, which was in operation in 1853-57.

United States of America
## REMINGTON ARMY MODEL 1863

Eliphalet Remington was originally a blacksmith but turned to gun-making fairly early in his career. He at first specialized in military rifles and soon gained an enviable reputation for the quality of the arms he produced. By 1857, he had begun to make a few pocket revolvers to a design made by F. Beals, but it was not until the outbreak of the American Civil War that he began to produce service revolvers in considerable quantity. The example illustrated is the improved Army Model of 1863; it was a fine arm in its day, perhaps its major feature being its solid frame, which gave it great rigidity. It has an octagonal barrel (the top flat inscribed "PATENTED SEP 14 1850 E REMINGTON AND SONS ILLION NEW YORK USA NEW MODEL") which screws into the frame, and a plain, six-shot cylinder with rectangular slots for the stop. The axis pin can be removed by drawing it forward. The lock is of the then customary single-action type and works smoothly; the act of cocking the hammer also rotates the cylinder. The rammer is of orthodox type; except that its lever broadens towards the rear, presumably to prevent it from catching on the holster, and gives it a streamlined appearance. The butt-plates are of very dark walnut. The trigger-guard, which is of brass, is rather small; it would not be easy to operate the trigger while wearing gloves. This handsome, well-made, service arm was used extensively by troops on the Union side during the Civil War and remained popular after the War was over.

United States of America
## STARR REVOLVER

The Starr Arms Company of New York began to manufacture revolvers of the kind seen here as a result of a patent of 15 January 1856. There were three types: a Navy double-action model of ·36" (9·1mm) calibre; a double-action Army model of ·44" (11·2mm) calibre; and a somewhat heavier, ·44" (11·2mm) calibre, single-action model, like the weapon illustrated here. Unlike the Colts of the period, the Starr has a top strap and the barrel is hinged at the front of the frame. The removal of the screw visible below the hammer nose (a task needing no tools) enables the revolver to be broken (rather like the later Webleys) and stripped for cleaning very easily. This particular arrangement makes it possible to dispense with a cylinder pin: the cylinder is mounted by means of its rear-projecting ratchet and by a forward plug fitting into recesses in the frame. The six-chambered cylinder is plain, except for 12 oval slots for the stop. These slots allow the cylinder to be locked with a nipple on either side of the nose of the hammer, thus eliminating the chance of accidental discharge by a drop or jolt. The rammer is of the powerful type usually found on such weapons. The one-piece walnut butt is held between two tangs. All the metalwork of the pistol is of steel. It has a blade foresight, adjustable laterally; the backsight is formed by a notch on the top of the nose of the hammer. This robust, well-made arm saw extensive use on the Union side in the Civil War and was also often carried by civilians as a belt pistol.

Great Britain
**BEAUMONT-ADAMS REVOLVER**

| | |
|---|---|
| **Length:** | 11·75" (298mm) |
| **Weight:** | 38oz (1·08kg) |
| **Barrel:** | 5·75" (146mm) |
| **Calibre:** | ·44" (11·2mm) |
| **Rifling:** | 3 groove, r/hand |
| **Capacity:** | Five |
| **Muz Vel:** | c550 f/s (168 m/s) |
| **Sights:** | Fixed |

Great Britain
**ADAMS SELF-COCKING REVOLVER**

| | |
|---|---|
| **Length:** | 11·5" (292mm) |
| **Weight:** | 30oz (·85kg) |
| **Barrel:** | 6·5" (165mm) |
| **Calibre:** | ·44" (11·2mm) |
| **Rifling:** | 3 groove, r/hand |
| **Capacity:** | Five |
| **Muz Vel:** | c550 f/s (168 m/s) |
| **Sights:** | Fixed |

Great Britain
**BEAUMONT-ADAMS REVOLVER**
Beaumont's double-action lock gave the user a choice of single action or self-cocking, and by the late 1850s Adams revolvers had probably overtaken Colt arms in the favour of British officers.

Great Britain
**ADAMS SELF-COCKING REVOLVER**
Note that the cylinder of this revolver—which is slightly unusual in that it revolves anti-clockwise—is appreciably shorter than that of the Beaumont-Adams revolver illustrated above.

Belgium
**COPY OF ADAMS REVOLVER**

| | |
|---|---|
| **Length:** | 13" (330mm) |
| **Weight:** | 33oz (·94kg) |
| **Barrel:** | 6·9" (175mm) |
| **Calibre:** | ·38" (9·6mm) |
| **Rifling:** | 8 groove, r/hand |
| **Capacity:** | Six |
| **Muz Vel:** | c500 f/s (152 m/s) |
| **Sights:** | Fixed |

Great Britain
**DEANE-HARDING REVOLVER**

| | |
|---|---|
| **Length:** | 12" (305mm) |
| **Weight:** | 41oz (1·16kg) |
| **Barrel:** | 5·25" (133mm) |
| **Calibre:** | ·44" (11·2mm) |
| **Rifling:** | 3 groove, r/hand |
| **Capacity:** | Five |
| **Muz Vel:** | c550 f/s (168 m/s) |
| **Sights:** | Fixed |

Belgium
**COPY OF ADAMS REVOLVER**
The ring trigger of this arm resembles those of earlier pepperbox pistols. Note the flat plate that shields the nipple under the hammer, protecting the firer from fragments of the percussion cap.

Great Britain
**DEANE-HARDING REVOLVER**
The Deane-Harding revolver was much criticised—Lord Roberts was quoted as saying that it could always be depended upon to malfunction at a critical moment—and never became popular.

Great Britain

## BEAUMONT-ADAMS REVOLVER

The original Adams revolvers of 1851 were self-cockers and thus could only be fired by quite heavy pressure on the trigger; this made them fast to use but somewhat inaccurate, except at close range. This deficiency was remedied in 1855 by the adoption of a double-action lock, the invention of Lieutenant F. Beaumont of the Royal Engineers. This allowed preliminary cocking for deliberate shooting, without affecting the rate of fire, and immediately became popular. It appears that only two calibres were made: the massive "Dragoon" arm (weighing 47oz/ 1.33kg, and of about ·49"/ 12·4mm calibre), and the smaller 54-bore (about ·44"/ 11·2mm calibre) revolver illustrated here. This weapon, while still having adequate stopping power, was of more manageable dimensions than the Dragoon, and was thus particularly favoured by unmounted officers, who had to carry their own revolvers. Like all Adams' weapons, the revolver is of strong construction. It has the usual one-piece frame with integral octagonal barrel, which is rifled and bears the foresight; the backsight is a simple notch on the frame above the standing breech. The plain cylinder, with its horizontal nipples separated by partitions, is somewhat longer than those of the original Adams, to allow for a heavier charge, and bears London proofmarks. There is a Kerr-type rammer on the left-hand side of the barrel. The lower frame is marked "B14886" and "Adams Patent No 30550 R", and carries an "L.A.C." (London Armoury Company) stamp.

Great Britain

## ADAMS SELF-COCKING REVOLVER

Adams revolvers attracted considerable attention at the Great Exhibition in London in 1851. Consequent demand may have taken the firm of Deane, Adams and Deane rather by surprise, for it was some time before the various arms came into full production. The original massive "Dragoon" type, 38-bore revolver was a bulky arm and, although suitable for mounted men, was rather too heavy for a man on foot. The revolver shown here is of the next size down and was of nominal 54-bore (about ·44"/11·2mm calibre). The word "nominal" is used deliberately, because some of the earliest models were, in fact, 56-bore and bear the small number "56" on the front of the frame: the weapon here is one such. It is of the usual strong, one-piece construction and its octagonal barrel is, of course, rifled. It bears the inscription "DEANE ADAMS AND DEANE, 30 KING WILLIAM STT, LONDON BRIDGE", and has London proofmarks. The cylinder, which is bright, has the usual five chambers and horizontal nipples separated by partitions. Unusually, it rotates in an anti-clockwise direction. The cylinder can be removed by first withdrawing the small plug on the upper end of the vertical spring on the front of the frame and then drawing the axis pin forward. The lock is of self-cocking type; there is a safety device to hold the hammer clear of the nipples on the left side of the frame. On this arm, no rammer is fitted; the bullets had oversized felt wads attached to their bases and were only thumb-tight in the chambers—this made for fast loading.

Belgium
## COPY OF ADAMS REVOLVER

Although Adams revolvers were made under licence in Belgium, the name on this pistol – "DAVID H. BREVETTE" – is not that of a licensee. The arm resembles those made by D. Herman of Liège and is probably a pirated copy. The frame is made separately from the octagonal barrel, which is attached to it Colt-fashion by means of a robust cylinder pin and a lump screwed to the lower part of the frame. A rammer, essentially similar to the type used on Beaumont-Adams revolvers, is attached to the left-hand flat of the barrel. The cylinder is of the normal Adams type and bears Liège proofmarks. The lock, too, is of the Adams self-cocking type; on the left-hand side is fitted a spring safety-bolt to hold the hammer clear of the nipples. A flat plate protrudes far enough forward from the top of the frame to cover completely the nipple under the hammer; this is presumably intended to remove any risk of fragments of the copper cap blowing back into the face of the firer. The trigger is of the ring type often found on pepperbox pistols.

*Officers of the 28th Bombay Native Infantry, Suakim Field Force, 1885. Adams revolvers were still in service use.*

Great Britain
## DEANE-HARDING REVOLVER

The Deane of the title of this arm is the older of Adams' two original partners. After severing the partnership, he continued to trade in firearms, and in 1858 began the manufacture of a new revolver patented in that year by William Harding. The weapon shown is of the popular 54-bore service calibre. Perhaps its main point of interest is the manner of its construction: the barrel, barrel lump and upper strap constitute a completely separate component from the frame. In order to strip the weapon, it is necessary first to remove the pin from the hole visible in front of the hammer nose. The barrel is then pushed downwards to an angle of 45°, which is sufficient to disengage a hook at the bottom of the lump from a corresponding socket in the lower frame. Various types of locking-pin were employed; in this specimen, the pin has been replaced by a screw, but this is a non-standard modification. The barrel group incorporates a rammer, which was also patented by Harding. When the lever below the barrel is released, by means of a spring, and pulled downward, a hook (concealed in the lump) draws the ram into the bottom chamber until the lever is vertically downwards. This method was efficient but is said to have been rather flimsy for service use. The lock is of double-action type, and the whole arm is broadly comparable to the Beaumont-Adams. It is difficult to assess the real value of the Deane-Harding arm; certainly, it attracted critical comment and never became popular.

Great Britain
**TRANTER REVOLVER, FIRST MODEL**

| | |
|---|---|
| **Length:** | 11·5" (292mm) |
| **Weight:** | 31oz (·88kg) |
| **Barrel:** | 6·5" (165mm) |
| **Calibre:** | ·44" (11·2mm) |
| **Rifling:** | 5 groove, r/hand |
| **Capacity:** | Five |
| **Muz Vel:** | c550 f/s (168 m/s) |
| **Sights:** | Fixed |

Great Britain
**TRANTER REVOLVER, SECOND MODEL**

| | |
|---|---|
| **Length:** | 11·5" (292mm) |
| **Weight:** | 29oz (·82kg) |
| **Barrel:** | 6·5" (165mm) |
| **Calibre:** | ·44" (11·2mm) |
| **Rifling:** | 5 groove, r/hand |
| **Capacity:** | Five |
| **Muz Vel:** | c550 f/s (168 m/s) |
| **Sights:** | Fixed |

Great Britain
**TRANTER REVOLVER, FIRST MODEL**
Tranter's first model was produced in a variety of calibres: 38-bore (·500"/12·7mm); 50-bore (·45"/11·4mm); 54-bore (·44"/11·2mm); 80-bore (·38"/9·6mm); 90-bore (·36"/9·1 mm); 120-bore (·32"/8·1mm).

Great Britain
**TRANTER REVOLVER, SECOND MODEL**
On the second model—which, like the third, appears to have been made only in the basic calibres of 38-, 54- and 120-bore—the rammer was semi-permanently attached to lessen the danger of loss.

Great Britain
**TRANTER REVOLVER, THIRD MODEL**

| | |
|---|---|
| **Length:** | 11·75" (298mm) |
| **Weight:** | 36oz (1·02kg) |
| **Barrel:** | 6" (152mm) |
| **Calibre:** | ·44" (11·2mm) |
| **Rifling:** | 5 groove, r/hand |
| **Capacity:** | Five |
| **Muz Vel:** | c550 f/s (168 m/s) |
| **Sights:** | Fixed |

Great Britain
**TRANTER REVOLVER, POCKET MODEL**

| | |
|---|---|
| **Length:** | 9·5" (241mm) |
| **Weight:** | 22oz (·62kg) |
| **Barrel:** | 4·3" (109mm) |
| **Calibre:** | ·38" (9·6mm) |
| **Rifling:** | 3 groove, r/hand |
| **Capacity:** | Five |
| **Muz Vel:** | c500 f/s (152 m/s) |
| **Sights:** | Fixed |

Great Britain
**TRANTER REVOLVER, THIRD MODEL**
The angle of the butt was changed in the third model. This conformed with a change made by Adams at the same time, and may thus confirm the supposition that Tranter manufactured frames for Adams.

Great Britain
**TRANTER REVOLVER, POCKET MODEL**
William Tranter, whose long career as a gunmaker lasted from 1840 to 1885, was particularly noted for his revolvers—both for percussion arms, like this pocket model, and cartridge revolvers.

Great Britain

## TRANTER REVOLVER, FIRST MODEL

William Tranter was a Birmingham gunmaker of the highest repute. Tranter realized that although self-cocking revolvers were excellent for fast shooting, their heavy trigger pull had an adverse effect on accuracy beyond point-blank range. He therefore set to work on a double-action lock and by 1853 had patented the weapon seen here—thus forestalling Beaumont. Pressure on the lower trigger (which is, in effect, a cocking lever) cocks the combless hammer; a very light pressure on the upper trigger is then sufficient to fire the shot. When speed was more important than accuracy, both triggers were pulled together, thus giving the fast shooting needed in a close-quarter mêlée. Tranter's revolvers were all fitted with rammers, and it is by the variations in these that the different models are identified. However, it must be clearly stated that the numbering of the models does not necessarily relate to the strict chronological order of their appearance. The weapon seen here is the first model: it is equipped with a detachable rammer, an example of which is shown below the arm. In order to use the rammer, it is necessary to put the ring on its end over a peg (visible) on the bottom of the frame and then raise the lever so that the ram bears on the bullet and forces it into the chamber. Round the base of each bullet was a cannelure, or groove, which contained a bees-wax mixture: the expansion of the bullet on firing forced bees-wax out into the bore, helping to reduce hard fouling and facilitating cleaning.

Great Britain

## TRANTER REVOLVER, SECOND MODEL

Although safe enough for target shooting, the fully detachable rammer of Tranter's first model was too easily lost on active service—and, because the bullets were tight-fitting, this prevented further use of the revolver. The rammer on the second model, seen here, therefore represents a compromise: it is so designed that it may be easily enough removed by aligning the recess on its ring with the pin protruding from its anchor peg, on the frame, and lifting it off. On the other hand, the fit was so good that the rammer could be left in position on the revolver without any risk of it falling off. In order to carry the loaded revolver in safety, it was, of course, necessary to keep the nose of the hammer clear of the caps on the nipples—and since the system precluded any use of the normal half-cock, some other device was needed. Tranter's solution was most ingenious: it consists of a spring in the shape of an inverted Y, which can be seen here on the left-hand side of the frame, behind the cylinder. When the hammer is slightly raised, a stud on the inside of the upper arm is interposed between the hammer and the nipples; it remains in position until pressure on the lower trigger brings the hammer back to full-cock, when it is automatically disengaged. This was a simple and effective device which, unlike the similar safety on the Adams, called for no conscious effort on the part of the firer to remove it before beginning to shoot. This revolver was much preferred to the version with easily-detachable rammer.

Great Britain
## TRANTER REVOLVER, THIRD MODEL

This third and final model of Tranter's double-trigger revolver again differs from the earlier ones because of its rammer, which, as may be seen, is in this arm firmly attached to the frame and is only to be removed by a screwdriver. The reasons for this change are not clear; it is possible that after long use the second type worked loose, to the stage where there was a risk of it falling off accidentally. It will be observed that in many essential features Tranter's revolvers bear a strong family resemblance to those of Adams. This is not surprising when it is considered that, until 1865, all frames for Tranter's revolvers were made under licence on an Adams patent, and were stamped accordingly. Tranter considered it essential to have the one-piece, malleable iron frame incorporating the barrel which was a major feature of Adams' arms—and he was content to pay a small royalty on each pistol for the privilege. It is, in fact, believed that Tranter, who was, it will be remembered, already a well-established gunsmith when Adams' revolver appeared, may have had a contract to make frames for Adams; at least, in the early days when Adams himself did not have the manufacturing capacity to cope with the demand. If this was so, the licence arrangement was clearly to Tranter's advantage, for he had the tools and expertise ready to hand in his own factory. When the patent expired in 1865, the system became common property and Tranter was able to continue to use it without further payment of a fee.

Great Britain
## TRANTER REVOLVER, POCKET MODEL

Tranter made revolvers in a variety of calibres: this pocket revolver of 80-bore (·38"/9·6mm) is the second model, with detachable rammer. Like others in this series, it conforms closely to the standard design and is fitted with the patent safety device and the usual cylinder axis retaining spring on the right-hand side. Like all Tranter's arms, it bears the inscription "W. TRANTER PATENT" on the upper trigger, just above the guard, and on the rammer, opposite the ram itself. It will be noted that the frame is of the later pattern, with raked-back butt; as it does not bear the words "Adams Patent", it must be presumed to have been made after the patent's expiry in 1865. It bears the usual light engraving on the sides of the frame and at the breech end of the barrel, the top flat of which is engraved "GASQUOINE AND DYSON, MARKET PLACE, MANCHESTER", this being the name of the retailer. This is in every respect a neat and compact weapon and, although a pocket pistol, it is of sufficient calibre to give it very reasonable stopping-power. A number of Tranter's revolvers were also made in Belgium under licence. Tranter took care to grant such licence only to reputable makers, with the result that the Belgian-made weapons are practically indistinguishable from the British ones, except that they bear an acknowledgement of the fact that they were made under a Tranter patent. Very occasionally, pocket Tranters may be encountered with a hinged lower trigger, which can be folded forward so as to lie flush outside the guard.

Germany
**PINFIRE REVOLVER**

| | |
|---|---|
| **Length:** | 11" (279mm) |
| **Weight:** | 27oz (·76kg) |
| **Barrel:** | 6" (152mm) |
| **Calibre:** | ·43" (11mm) |
| **Rifling:** | 5 groove, l/hand |
| **Capacity:** | Six |
| **Muz Vel:** | c600 f/s (183 m/s) |
| **Sights:** | Fixed |

France
**PINFIRE REVOLVER**

| | |
|---|---|
| **Length:** | 8·4" (213mm) |
| **Weight:** | 20oz (·56kg) |
| **Barrel:** | 4" (102mm) |
| **Calibre:** | ·35" (9mm) |
| **Rifling:** | 4 groove, r/hand |
| **Capacity:** | Six |
| **Muz Vel:** | c600 f/s (183 m/s) |
| **Sights:** | Fixed |

Germany
**PINFIRE REVOLVER**
Note the apertures running from the chambers to the rear edge of the cylinder. The pinfire cartridges must be inserted into the chambers so that their pins project from these apertures.

France
**PINFIRE REVOLVER**
The trigger of this Lefaucheux-type pinfire revolver folds forward, so that the arm may be more easily carried in a pocket.

France
**FIST PISTOL**

| | |
|---|---|
| **Length:** | 4·8" (122mm) |
| **Weight:** | 11oz (·31kg) |
| **Barrel:** | 1·9" (48mm) |
| **Calibre:** | ·275" (7mm) |
| **Rifling:** | Nil |
| **Capacity:** | Six |
| **Muz Vel:** | c450 f/s (137 m/s) |
| **Sights:** | Nil |

Germany
**PINFIRE REVOLVER**

| | |
|---|---|
| **Length:** | 10·4" (264mm) |
| **Weight:** | 26oz (·73kg) |
| **Barrel:** | 5·4" (137mm) |
| **Calibre:** | ·35" (9mm) |
| **Rifling:** | 6 groove, r/hand |
| **Capacity:** | Six |
| **Muz Vel:** | c550 f/s (168 m/s) |
| **Sights:** | Fixed |

France
**FIST PISTOL**
As reference to the photographs on pages 16-17 will show, this arm is by definition a pepperbox. Weapons of this type sometimes incorporated a knuckleduster and dagger, and when thus equipped they were called "Apache pistols"—a reference to the infamous denizens of the underworld of 19th-century Paris.

Germany
**PINFIRE REVOLVER**
Note the pinfire cartridge. The hammer strikes the pin, driving it inward to set off the percussion cap in the base of the cartridge.

Germany
## PINFIRE REVOLVER

A pinfire cartridge is shown with the lower revolver on page 41. From that example, it will be seen that the pinfire cartridge consisted of a rimless, cylindrical, brass case containing the charge; a bullet; and, most important of all, an internal percussion cap inserted into a small compartment in the cartridge's base. The inner end of the small brass-wire pin rested on this cap. When it was driven inwards by the blow of the hammer, it set off the cap and fired the charge. Apertures run from the chambers to the rear edge of the cylinder. To load the revolver, it was necessary to open the top-hinged loading gate; place the hammer at half-cock; and insert the cartridges into the chambers in such a way that the pins protruded from the apertures. The hammer was so shaped that when it fell it struck the outer end of the pin and thus fired the cartridge. The thin brass case expanded at this instant and prevented any rearward escape of burning gases. Then the metal's natural elasticity caused it to contract, so that it could be easily removed by the sliding rod below the barrel.

France
## PINFIRE REVOLVER

Perfection of the percussion system made possible a self-contained cartridge for breech loading weapons. But it was difficult to obtain perfect obturation—ie, preventing burning gases escaping from the breech at the moment of firing—without a breech mechanism so complex that it offered little advantage over muzzle-loaders. Casimir Lefaucheux invented the pinfire cartridge in 1828 and it was in fairly extensive use on the continent by 1840. But it did not seem to arouse much interest in Britain until shown with a pepperbox-type arm at the Great Exhibition of 1851. Then Casimir's son Eugène patented a more modern arm in Britain in 1854. As seen, it is plain and robust. The octagonal barrel is attached to the axis pin and is further braced against the lower frame, making a reasonably rigid joint. The heavy standing breech incorporates a top-hinged loading gate with a spring catch. A sliding rod is provided to knock out empty cases. Small, square studs on the otherwise plain cylinder engage with the stop to hold the cylinder rigid at the moment of firing.

*French sailors in c1870 drill with what appear to be Lefaucheux pinfire revolvers.*

France
## FIST PISTOL

It was with a pistol of this type – known as a *coup de poing* in France – that Lefaucheux exhibited his pinfire cartridge in 1851. It is a rather ugly little weapon. Its long, fluted, pepperbox cylinder is made from a single piece of metal, and the front end of the cylinder axis pin is supported by a bracket screwed to the front end of the lower frame. The standing breech consists of a flat, circular plate: a semi-circular portion is cut out on the right-hand side so that the weapon can be loaded from the breech end. This loading aperture is filled by a bottom-hinged gate fitted with a small stud to give purchase; and its bottom end bears on the small, horizontal, L-shaped spring screwed below it on the frame. There is a further shallow depression, into which the hammer fits, on top of the standing breech. The lock is of self-cocking type and can only be fired by steady pressure on the trigger, which is of the forward-hinged variety and is thus without a trigger-guard. The cylinder is normally free to rotate, but when the trigger is pressed a cylinder-stop rises from the lower frame and engages one of the studs which can be seen on the cylinder. When loaded, the cylinder may be positioned so that there is a pin on either side of the hammer head, thus making it relatively safe to carry the loaded weapon in a pocket. Once the rounds have been fired, the empty cases may be pushed out through the open loading gate by means of a separate extractor pin. This is screwed into the base of the butt when not in use: its end is visible in the arm seen here.

Germany
## PINFIRE REVOLVER

This is an attractive arm, strong and well-made, as one would expect of a German weapon, and of unusually good quality and finish. It has a one-piece frame with a top strap and an octagonal barrel, on which the top flat is narrowed to form a distinct rib. It has an unusually high (and thus, perhaps, slightly vulnerable) foresight, while the backsight is a V-shaped notch on the rear of the top strap. The cylinder is unfluted and has long and elegantly-formed projections: these engage against the cylinder stop, which rises from the lower frame when the trigger is pressed. It is fitted with the usual loading gate, with a thumb piece and a spring catch projecting below it. This holds the gate firmly in position, yet allows it to be opened with quite light thumb pressure. The cylinder is removed by pulling forward the axis pin, and on the left-hand side of the frame is a vertical spring and stud which prevents accidental removal. The lock is of double-action type: the arm can be fired either by simple trigger pressure, or by preliminary cocking of the hammer, according to circumstances. There is an upward bulge at the rear end of the top strap to prevent the protruding pins from fouling it when the cylinder rotates, and there is a corresponding notch on the bottom of the frame. The pistol is well blued and engraved, with the exception of the hammer, trigger, foresight and ejector rod, which are of bright steel. The one-piece butt is held by two tangs. The top strap bears the inscription "J A COSTER IN HANAU", and there is a gold monogram on the top tang.

Great Britain
**TRANTER RIMFIRE REVOLVER**

| | |
|---|---|
| **Length:** | 12" (305mm) |
| **Weight:** | 50oz (1·4kg) |
| **Barrel:** | 6·5" (165mm) |
| **Calibre:** | ·45" (11·4mm) |
| **Rifling:** | 5 groove, r/hand |
| **Capacity:** | Six |
| **Muz Vel:** | c650 f/s (198 m/s) |
| **Sights:** | Fixed |

United States of America
**ALLEN AND WHEELOCK REVOLVER**

| | |
|---|---|
| **Length:** | 8" (203mm) |
| **Weight:** | 15oz (·43kg) |
| **Barrel:** | 4" (102mm) |
| **Calibre:** | ·32" (8·1mm) |
| **Rifling:** | 6 groove, l/hand |
| **Capacity:** | Six |
| **Muz Vel:** | c500 f/s (152 m/s) |
| **Sights:** | Fixed |

Great Britain
**TRANTER RIMFIRE REVOLVER**
Note the rammer lever lying along the barrel: when it is pulled downward, the ram is forced through a sleeve into the chamber.

United States of America
**ALLEN AND WHEELOCK REVOLVER**
A product of the partnership of Ethan Allen (maker of the pepperbox illustrated on page 16) and Thomas P. Wheelock, this cheaply-made rimfire revolver has a sheathed trigger. The absence of a trigger guard makes it more convenient for use as a pocket weapon.

United States of America
**SMITH AND WESSON TIP-UP REVOLVER**

| | |
|---|---|
| **Length:** | 10" (254mm) |
| **Weight:** | 21oz (·6kg) |
| **Barrel:** | 5" (127mm) |
| **Calibre:** | ·32" (8·1mm) |
| **Rifling:** | 6 groove, r/hand |
| **Capacity:** | Six |
| **Muz Vel:** | c600 f/s (182 m/s) |
| **Sights:** | Fixed |

Europe
**CONTINENTAL TIP-UP REVOLVER**

| | |
|---|---|
| **Length:** | 10·75" (273mm) |
| **Weight:** | 32oz (·9kg) |
| **Barrel:** | 5·5" (140mm) |
| **Calibre:** | ·44" (11·2mm) |
| **Rifling:** | 7 groove, r/hand |
| **Capacity:** | Five |
| **Muz Vel:** | c600 f/s (183 m/s) |
| **Sights:** | Fixed |

United States of America
**SMITH AND WESSON TIP-UP REVOLVER**
Note the pins on top of the frame, securing the cylinder stop. These gave this weapon—called by its makers the Model No 2 (Army) —the unofficial designation of the "three-pin" revolver.

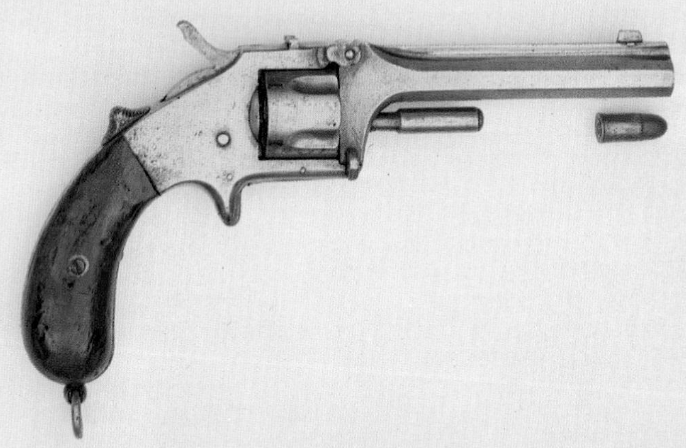

Europe
**CONTINENTAL TIP-UP REVOLVER**
The size of this revolver and the fact that it is fitted with a lanyard ring suggest that it was intended for military use.

Great Britain

## TRANTER RIMFIRE REVOLVER

The name of Tranter has already been mentioned several times in this book in connection with the early double-trigger percussion revolvers for which he is perhaps best known. Apart from these, however, Tranter also produced a good many double-action percussion revolvers, in a variety of sizes, in order to compete with Beaumont-Adams arms, especially military arms in service calibres. Once the popularity of the new Smith and Wesson breechloading revolvers was assured, Tranter, a competent and enterprising individual, wasted little time: by 1863 he had placed on the market the rimfire revolver seen here. This was the first of its type to be produced (or, it might be safer to say, acknowledged) by a British maker. Reference back to the percussion section will show its continuing strong resemblance to the Adams arms: indeed Tranter had used the Adams frame, under licence, for his revolvers. The cylinder (which is, of course, bored through) has six chambers instead of the five customary in Tranter's earlier models; and the rear ends of the chambers are recessed to accommodate the rims of the cartridges. There is a bottom-hinged loading gate on the right-hand side of the standing breech. The rammer lever, which is inscribed "TRANTERS PATENT", acts downwards, forcing the ram into the chamber through a sleeve. It is a close fit, in order to push out the cases by their forward edges. This meant that chamber and ram had to be most carefully aligned

United States of America

## ALLEN AND WHEELOCK REVOLVER

When Smith and Wesson produced a tip-up revolver with the Rollin White bored-through cylinder and their patent rimfire cartridge, both aspects of the arm were fully protected in the USA. Its novelty and utility made it most susceptible to piracy, and Smith and Wesson took action against many makers—among them Allen and Wheelock, makers of this weapon. Rollin White began proceedings in 1859 but was not successful until 1863. This revolver has a solid frame, including the butt, into which an octagonal barrel is screwed. There are no facilities either for loading the revolver or ejecting the empty cases with the cylinder in position. To do so it is necessary first to remove the large-headed screw below the front frame, which allows the cylinder axis pin to be drawn forward and the cylinder removed. Empty cases may then be punched out by the axis pin; the chambers reloaded, if necessary; and the cylinder replaced. This made the revolver very slow to reload, but it also greatly simplified manufacture and thus made it cheap to produce. The weapon has a single-action lock with an external hammer on the right-hand side, access to the mechanism being gained by way of an oval inspection plate on the left. The trigger is of the variety known as "sheathed"; it has no trigger-guard, and this reduces its bulk and makes it a suitable pocket arm. The barrel and frame are crudely engraved with a standing pugilist on the right side and a kneeling one on the left, with a further motif of boxing gloves on the inspection plate cover.

United States of America

## SMITH AND WESSON TIP-UP REVOLVER

In 1855 an American inventor named Rollin White patented a revolver with a bored-through cylinder. When the firm of Smith and Wesson began to consider the production of a modern cartridge revolver (which they would be able to do as soon as Colt's patent for a revolving cylinder expired in 1857) they had the good sense to buy this patent. This gave them a monopoly on the system in the United States, although it did not apply to Europe. The first pistols incorporating the system—of ·22in (5·6mm) calibre, firing copper rimfire cartridges—were on the market in 1858. They quickly became popular and several variations were developed. The revolver seen here is the Model No 2 (Army); this became available in 1861 and was widely purchased as a private arm during the Civil War. The octagonal barrel is hinged to the front of the top frame, and a retaining catch holds it to the lower frame. When the catch is pushed upward, the barrel can be raised and the cylinder removed, the empty cases being pushed out by means of the pin below the barrel. The cylinder stop is a flat spring on top of the frame; it is held by two pins, and is lifted clear of the cylinder by the hammer nose. The extra forward pin is said to have been added to strengthen the stop: the model is thus usually known as the "three-pin". It was made in a variety of barrel lengths, the longest being six inches (152mm) and the shortest four inches (102mm). The Model No 2 (Army) remained popular into the 1870s, and total production amounted to more than 77,000 revolvers.

Europe

## CONTINENTAL TIP-UP REVOLVER

The invention of the self-contained metallic cartridge led to a great upsurge of interest in revolvers. The earliest of these new cartridges was, perhaps, the pinfire. It was soon followed by a cartridge made of copper and having a rim with a compound of fulminate of mercury inserted beneath it. When the outer side of the soft copper base was struck by a hammer, the blow was sufficient to detonate the internal fulminate and fire the charge. This system made possible the development of a self-contained cartridge of material sufficiently elastic for it to be expanded by the pressure of the gases at the instant of firing, thus avoiding the rearward leakage of gases which had been a problem with earlier breechloaders. The cartridge had the added advantages of being watertight and having no protruding pin; so it soon became popular. Smith and Wesson patented a ·22in (5·6mm) cartridge of this type in the United States in 1855-56. But the company's patent for a bored-through cylinder was valid only in the USA and gave them no protection against copyists elsewhere. The revolver illustrated is a European copy, dated 1874 on the left-hand side of the barrel frame, and with two manufacturing numbers on the cylinder. The major differences (apart from size) from the genuine arm are the provision of a backsight on the top frame; the fact that the cylinder stop rises from the bottom; and the fact that the weapon is of centre-fire rather than rimfire type and is fitted with a sliding safety catch behind the hammer.

France
**LAGRESE REVOLVER**

| | |
|---|---|
| **Length:** | 11·75" (298mm) |
| **Weight:** | 28oz (·79kg) |
| **Barrel:** | 6·25" (159mm) |
| **Calibre:** | ·43" (10·9mm) |
| **Rifling:** | 8 groove, l/hand |
| **Capacity:** | Six |
| **Muz Vel:** | c550 f/s (168 m/s) |
| **Sights:** | Fixed |

Great Britain
**TRANTER POCKET REVOLVER**

| | |
|---|---|
| **Length:** | 8" (203mm) |
| **Weight:** | 19oz (·54kg) |
| **Barrel:** | 3·5" (89mm) |
| **Calibre:** | ·32" (8·1mm) |
| **Rifling:** | 5 groove, r/hand |
| **Capacity:** | Seven |
| **Muz Vel:** | c550 f/s (168 m/s) |
| **Sights:** | Fixed |

France
**LAGRESE REVOLVER**
This is a large and complex arm of somewhat eccentric design. Note the quite perceptible gap (in fact, about ·05"/1·3mm) between the barrel and the cylinder, which must have led to a considerable escape of gases, and the upward-acting rammer of percussion type.

Great Britain
**TRANTER POCKET REVOLVER**
This pocket revolver of good quality is chambered for seven rimfire cartridges. The centre-fire cartridge quickly ousted the rimfire type in revolvers of service calibre, but the older cartridge remained in use in pocket arms for many years.

Great Britain
**ADAMS REVOLVER CONVERSION**

| | |
|---|---|
| **Length:** | 11·5" (292mm) |
| **Weight:** | 33oz (·94kg) |
| **Barrel:** | 6·5" (165mm) |
| **Calibre:** | ·44" (11·2mm) |
| **Rifling:** | 3 groove, r/hand |
| **Capacity:** | Five |
| **Muz Vel:** | c550 f/s (168 m/s) |
| **Sights:** | Fixed |

France
**DEVISME REVOLVER**

| | |
|---|---|
| **Length:** | 12·5" (317mm) |
| **Weight:** | 32oz (·91kg) |
| **Barrel:** | 5·75" (146mm) |
| **Calibre:** | ·41" (10·4mm) |
| **Rifling:** | 4 groove, l/hand |
| **Capacity:** | Six |
| **Muz Vel:** | c550 f/s (168 m/s) |
| **Sights:** | Fixed |

Great Britain
**ADAMS REVOLVER CONVERSION**
The most noticeable differences between this arm and the original percussion model (see page 32, bottom) are the addition of the loading gate and its spring and the ejector rod and its sleeve.

France
**DEVISME REVOLVER**
A high-quality arm, this revolver is notable also for fine finish, with barrel and cylinder blued and the remainder case-hardened. The maker's name is visible on the frame just forward of the cylinder.

France

## LAGRESE REVOLVER

This revolver, made by Lagrese of Paris in about 1866, is well made and finished; but, as may be seen from the photograph, it is of somewhat ornate appearance and extreme complexity. The frame, including the butt, is made in one piece without any top strap; the octagonal barrel is screwed to the front end of the frame through which also passes the cylinder axis pin. This appears to make a rigid joint and there is no play apparent—although the permanent gap between the barrel and the cylinder is about ·05in (1·3mm), which must have led to a considerable loss of gases. The arrangement of the cylinder is also strange. It is fitted with a separate back plate which incorporates a loading gate. Conical apertures are pierced through the back plate to allow the nose of the hammer to reach the cartridges. In order to load, it is necessary first to put the nose of the hammer into a safety hole in the plate. This holds the plate rigid but allows the gate to be opened and the cylinder to be rotated clockwise. A groove on the right side of the butt allows the rounds to be slid in. The ejection is of percussion rammer type, in which an upward pull of the lever forces the ram backwards into the chamber. The lock is of the self-cocking variety, but there is a basic comb on the hammer which allows it to be drawn back slightly and then lowered into the safety hole mentioned earlier. The arm is lightly engraved but there are no traces at all of any finish. The barrel is inscribed "Lagrese Bte a Paris". All in all, this is a truly remarkable weapon.

Great Britain

## TRANTER POCKET REVOLVER

At first, revolvers formed only a small part of William Tranter's output, but after the American Civil War, when trade in service-type weapons fell away badly, he probably produced more revolvers, particularly pocket models, than any other UK manufacturer. The arm shown is fairly typical of his work. It has a solid and robust frame, into which the barrel is screwed, and a plain, seven-shot cylinder with recesses to accommodate the cartridge rims. The cylinder is rotated by a pawl, worked by the hammer, acting on a ratchet; the latter is cut out of the actual cylinder instead of attached to it. The cylinder stop rises from the bottom of the frame and engages the rectangular slots towards the front of the cylinder. The cylinder pin is retained by a small, vertical spring: pressure on the bottom end of the spring allows the pin to be withdrawn. The weapon has a bottom-hinged loading gate on the right-hand side of the frame into which a groove has been machined to allow the copper rimfire cartridges to be inserted. No ejector is fitted: to unload, it is necessary either to use the cylinder pin or to lever the cases out by inserting a knife-point or small screwdriver into the wide slots around the rear edge of the cylinder. This was a somewhat slow method; but presumably it was felt that seven rounds in the cylinder would usually be ample for self-defence. The lock, which is of single-action type, is fitted with a half-cock and is operated by the sheathed trigger usual on pocket arms. The weapon is marked "TRANTERS PATENT" on the frame.

Great Britain

## ADAMS REVOLVER CONVERSION

The revolver seen here was originally an Adams self-cocking, percussion arm, and it has been converted to a breechloader to take centre-fire cartridges. As will be seen by comparison with the Adams arm on page 32 (bottom) the basic conversion was a fairly simple one. The weapon has been fitted with a bored-through, five-chambered cylinder; this, in turn, necessitated the fitting of a loading gate, which can be seen on the right-hand side. The gate is hinged at the bottom and opens backwards. Its bottom end is supported on a flat spring screwed to the lower part of the frame; the pressure of the spring holds the gate firmly open or closed, as required. A piece of metal of the required shape has been screwed to the left-hand side of the frame to prevent the cartridges slipping out, and has been carefully fitted in front of the spring safety which holds the hammer clear of the rounds. The only other addition is a simple ejector rod working in a sleeve, which has been brazed on to the frame. No change has been made to the lock, which remains on the self-cocking principle. The lower flat of the barrel is engraved "P. W. ADAIR COLDSTREAM GUARDS"; an upper flat is engraved "CRIMEA, SEBASTOPOL"—a campaign in which Captain Adair served and in which, presumably, he carried this revolver. He was later in his career appointed Colonel-Commandant of the 4th (Militia) Battalion of the Somerset Light Infantry. Adams conversions were adopted by the British Army in 1868 and remained in official British service use until 1880.

France

## DEVISME REVOLVER

The manufacturer of this weapon was F. P. Devisme, a Parisian gunmaker of considerable repute, who had produced a self-cocking percussion revolver in limited quantity before 1830. He was also an early experimenter with centre-fire cartridges. The revolver seen here is of the type first shown at the Paris Exhibition of 1867, and it is fairly closely based on an earlier percussion revolver by the same maker. It has a cylindrical steel barrel screwed into a frame which is, in turn, hinged at the bottom of the standing breech, just in front of the trigger-guard. Pressure on the vertical milled lever in front of the frame allows the barrel to drop down to an angle of about 45°, giving access to the cylinder. The locking device is somewhat unusual, for it is based on the cylinder axis pin. The front end of the pin passes through the frame and is attached to the opening lever. The rear end has on it a rectangular stud which enters a corresponding socket on the standing breech when the arm is closed. Returning the opening lever to its normal, vertical position causes the stud to turn in the socket and locks it firmly. The extractor pin sleeve is attached to another sleeve round the barrel: the movement of the lever activates a simple rack-and-pinion device which swings the extractor pin out to the right, in readiness to knock out the empty cases one at a time. The lock is of single-action type and is fitted with a half-cock to hold the hammer nose clear of the rounds in the chambers. The weapon is of excellent quality and finish.

Great Britain
**THOMAS REVOLVER**

| | |
|---|---|
| **Length:** | 10·75" (273mm) |
| **Weight:** | 31oz (·88kg) |
| **Barrel:** | 5·75" (146mm) |
| **Calibre:** | ·45" (11·4mm) |
| **Rifling:** | 7 groove, l/hand |
| **Capacity:** | Five |
| **Muz Vel:** | c600 f/s (183 m/s) |
| **Sights:** | Fixed |

Great Britain
**HILL'S SELF-EXTRACTING REVOLVER**

| | |
|---|---|
| **Length:** | 7·75" (197mm) |
| **Weight:** | 15oz (·43kg) |
| **Barrel:** | 3·75" (95mm) |
| **Calibre:** | ·32" (8·1mm) |
| **Rifling:** | 7 groove, r/hand |
| **Capacity:** | Six |
| **Muz Vel:** | c550 f/s (168 m/s) |
| **Sights:** | Fixed |

Great Britain
**THOMAS REVOLVER**
The apparently complex extractor system devised for this revolver was effective enough—but was soon replaced by better ones. Thus, arms incorporating it were made in small numbers and are now rare.

Great Britain
**HILL'S SELF-EXTRACTING REVOLVER**
There is some doubt as to whether W.J. Hill of Birmingham actually invented the self-extracting mechanism used in this arm, for the same system is also found on revolvers of continental origin.

Great Britain
**TIP-UP REVOLVER**

| | |
|---|---|
| **Length:** | 8·5" (216mm) |
| **Weight:** | 21oz (·59kg) |
| **Barrel:** | 4" (102mm) |
| **Calibre:** | ·38" (9·6mm) |
| **Rifling:** | 5 groove, r/hand |
| **Capacity:** | Six |
| **Muz Vel:** | c600 f/s (183 m/s) |
| **Sights:** | Fixed |

Belgium
**GALAND AND SOMMERVILLE REVOLVER**

| | |
|---|---|
| **Length:** | 10" (254mm) |
| **Weight:** | 35oz (·99kg) |
| **Barrel:** | 5" (127mm) |
| **Calibre:** | ·45" (11·4mm) |
| **Rifling:** | 5 groove, r/hand |
| **Capacity:** | Six |
| **Muz Vel:** | c600 f/s (183 m/s) |
| **Sights:** | Fixed |

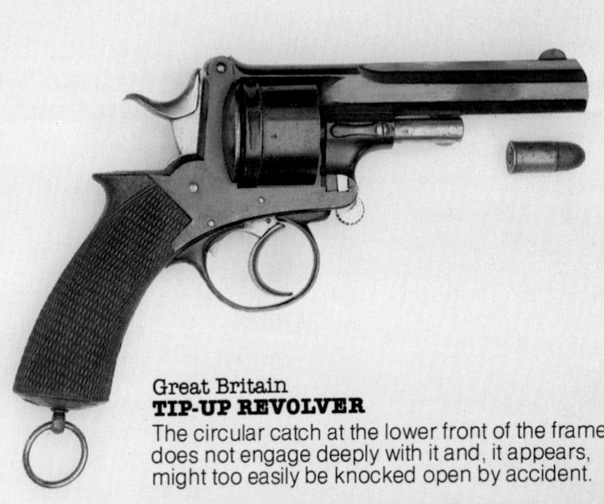

Great Britain
**TIP-UP REVOLVER**
The circular catch at the lower front of the frame does not engage deeply with it and, it appears, might too easily be knocked open by accident.

Belgium
**GALAND AND SOMMERVILLE REVOLVER**
The revolver is opened and the self-extracting mechanism activated by gripping the milled studs at the bottom of the frame and pulling forward. This forces back the plunger visible below the barrel.

Great Britain

## THOMAS REVOLVER

Loading an early cartridge revolver was a slow process, and efforts were soon made to improve it. In 1869, J. Thomas, a Birmingham gunmaker, patented this revolver. This weapon is of cast steel with a heavy octagonal barrel. Its main features of note are its very long cylinder aperture and the knob beneath its barrel. The revolver is loaded in the normal way, through the loading gate behind the right-hand end of the cylinder, and it is discharged by means of its double-action lock. The real point of interest is the system by which the empty cases are ejected. Pressure on the end of a small spring on the front of the frame releases the barrel catch and allows the barrel to be rotated until the knob (which is there simply to give a firm hold to a hot or oily hand) is uppermost. Then the barrel is drawn forward, taking the cylinder with it to the front of the aperture. A star-shaped extractor is attached to the standing breech, which holds the cases firmly by their rims until they are fully out of the chambers. Then they are thrown clear by a flick of the wrist; the barrel and cylinder are turned back; and the revolver is reloaded in the usual way. What is not apparent from the illustration (although the end of it can just be seen) is the provision on the barrel of a flange working in a slot on the frame. This flange is set at a slight angle to the circumference of the barrel: when the latter is turned it exerts a powerful camming action and draws the cylinder very slightly forward, thus loosening the tightest of cases.

Great Britain

## HILL'S SELF-EXTRACTING REVOLVER

Although the metallic cartridge was a valuable innovation, the system of reloading the earliest types of cartridge revolver was slow. It was necessary first to put the hammer at half-cock; open the loading gate; swing out the pin (if it was not already in alignment); and push out the empty cases one by one before loading new rounds. In this tip-up revolver by W. J. Hill of Birmingham, dating from c1880, no special manual operation is necessary to eject the empty cases. There are two hinges: one where the top frame is attached to the standing breech (its pivot pin can be seen); and a second where the barrel joins the frame. The pivot pin of the latter is also visible in the crescent-shaped lever, although the joint itself is concealed behind it. In order to open the weapon, it is necessary first to press the flat lever (just visible) on the lower front corner of the frame and raise the barrel. At this stage, the front hinge remains rigid and only the rear one opens. When the barrel is vertical, the limit of the rear hinge is reached and the crescent-shaped lever also locks. Continued pressure on the barrel causes the front hinge to come into play, allowing the barrel to continue backwards beyond the vertical. Now, the small stud which protrudes from the front of the frame, and is attached to the extractor rod, bears on the front end of the crescent and is thrust downward, so pushing out the star extractor and the empty case. The barrel is marked "HILLS PATENT SELF-EXTRACTOR", although there is some doubt as to whether Hill himself actually invented it.

Great Britain
## TIP-UP REVOLVER

The weapon seen here is an example of yet another attempt to speed up the reloading rate of a cartridge revolver. Although of good quality, it bears no maker's name; but its general style and its London proofmarks indicate that it is of British origin. It is a cartridge revolver of the tip-up type: upward pressure on the circular catch at the lower front of the frame allows the barrel to be raised to the vertical. Then, the very thick ejector pin—which is, in fact, shaped with a right-angled knob like an ordinary door bolt—is first rotated as far as possible, exerting a powerful camming action on the star-shaped extractor, and then pushed sharply backwards, thus thrusting out the extractor with its empty cases. The general principle is a sound one and foreshadows the introduction of the tip-down revolver with its automatic ejector. Its main weakness appears to lie in the catch, which does not engage deeply with the frame and might open accidentally.

Belgium
## GALAND AND SOMMERVILLE REVOLVER

Charles François Galand was a gunmaker of Liège in Belgium; Sommerville was a partner in a Birmingham firm. In 1868, they took out a joint patent for a self-extracting cartridge revolver of the general type illustrated, and the arm was made thereafter in Birmingham and on the continent. It does not appear ever to have become popular in Great Britain, but a good many revolvers on this principle were made in Europe. This particular specimen is well made but is unnamed, although it carries the name "Wm POWELL of BIRMINGHAM", who was probably the retailer. It bears Birmingham proof marks, and somewhat unusually, an Enfield Small Arms mark of crossed lances with a "B" beneath them. The revolver is opened by gripping the milled studs at the bottom of the frame and drawing them forward. This activates a plunger below the barrel (very like the ram on a percussion revolver) and forces both barrel and cylinder forward, leaving the empty cases held by their rims on the extractor. The partial return of the cylinder to the extractor allows fresh rounds to be loaded.

*The Galand revolver is opened to extract empty cases. Note position of lever and the star extractor on the axis pin.*

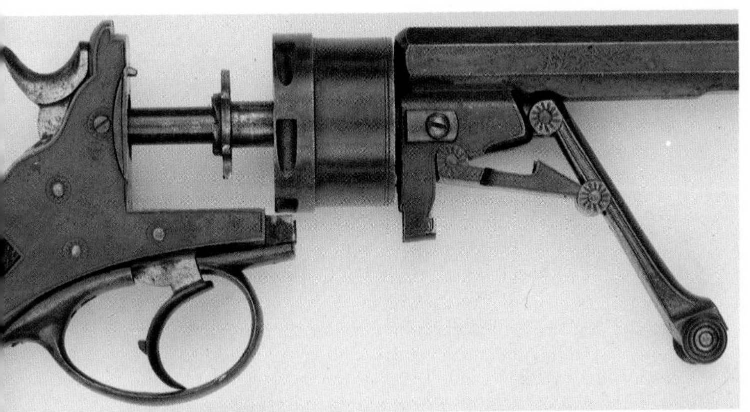

Great Britain
**WEBLEY No 1 REVOLVER**

| | |
|---|---|
| **Length:** | 9·5" (241mm) |
| **Weight:** | 42oz (1·19kg) |
| **Barrel:** | 5" (127mm) |
| **Calibre:** | ·577" (14·6mm) |
| **Rifling:** | 7 groove, r/hand |
| **Capacity:** | Six |
| **Muz Vel:** | c600 f/s (183 m/s) |
| **Sights:** | Fixed |

Great Britain
**WEBLEY No 1 REVOLVER**
This massive centre-fire revolver was adopted for British service use in 1872. It was designed (by John Adams, brother of the more famous Robert) to provide stopping-power against the fanatical and powerfully-built adversaries encountered in colonial warfare.

In the stripped Webley No 1 revolver, note particularly the notched backplate, with expansion holes for the primers.

Great Britain
**BLAND-PRYSE TYPE REVOLVER**

| | |
|---|---|
| **Length:** | 11·5" (292mm) |
| **Weight:** | 46oz (1·3kg) |
| **Barrel:** | 6·25" (159mm) |
| **Calibre:** | ·577" (14·6mm) |
| **Rifling:** | 5 groove, r/hand |
| **Capacity:** | Five |
| **Muz Vel:** | 650 f/s (198 m/s) |
| **Sights:** | Fixed |

France
**LE MAT REVOLVER**

| | |
|---|---|
| **Length:** | 10·2" (259mm) |
| **Weight:** | 49oz (1·39kg) |
| **Barrel:** | 4·6" (117mm) |
| **Calibre:** | ·44/·65" (11·2/16·5mm) |
| **Rifling:** | 5 groove, l/hand |
| **Capacity:** | Nine/One |
| **Muz Vel:** | c600 f/s (183 m/s) |
| **Sights:** | Fixed |

Great Britain
**BLAND-PRYSE TYPE REVOLVER**
When the milled discs on the ends of the arms behind the cylinder are pressed, inward-facing studs on the arms' upper ends disengage from the rear extension of the top frame. The revolver then opens on the hinge at the bottom front of the frame.

France
**LE MAT REVOLVER**
The earlier, percussion version of this massive arm invented by Dr Jean Alexandre Le Mat, a French resident in the USA, was called the "grape-shot" revolver—a reference to the supposed efficacy of its lower shot barrel in close-quarter combat.

Great Britain

## WEBLEY No 1 REVOLVER

In 1866 the British government approved the adoption of a breechloading rifle. This was the original Enfield percussion arm, converted by the addition of the Snider breech mechanism. In fact, the rifle caused a good deal of trouble until Colonel E. M. Boxer, Superintendent of the Royal Laboratory at Woolwich Arsenal, produced a workable (although by no means perfect) round for it. This had a cast-iron base, with an aperture for the copper percussion cap, to which was cemented a body of coiled brass foil. Soon after its adoption, the government approved in principle the issue of a revolver to fire a similar type of cartridge. The arm finally selected was invented by John Adams (brother of the more famous Robert) but was not finally adopted until 1872. In the meantime, the well-known firm of P. Webley and Son stepped in and produced a centre-fire revolver of its own, presumably in the hope of securing the market. Rimfire revolvers made by Tranter and others were already available, but British officers (who in those days bought their own revolvers) naturally liked to keep up-to-date, for their lives might depend on their having the best personal weapon available. Experience during the Indian Mutiny had shown that small, high-velocity bullets lacked the sheer knock-down power necessary to stop a charging fanatic dead in his tracks, so Webley's first centre-fire revolver was designed specifically so that it would not fail its user in that respect. The Webley No 1 revolver, illustrated here, was of ·577in (14·6mm) calibre, exactly the same as that of the service rifle. Although it is, perhaps, difficult to appreciate the fact from a photograph, one's first reaction on seeing the arm is to wonder at its massive construction. The revolver is built on a robust solid frame with integral barrel. As in many Webley products of the period, the barrel (although in this example octagonal) is noticeably higher from bottom to top than from side to side. This is particularly true of the muzzle-end; even in a short barrel the taper is quite obvious. The cylinder is fully fluted and the lock is of double-action type. One of the problems connected with the early Boxer cartridge was a marked tendency for the primer to bulge backwards under the force of the explosion. In some forms of breech mechanism, this was not particularly important; but in a revolver of orthodox type—ie, one in which the base of the cartridge was forced back against a robust standing breech—there was always the risk that a bulged primer would prevent the cylinder from rotating. Obviously, if this should happen at a critical moment it might have very serious results for the user. The Webley No 1 was therefore fitted with a detachable back-plate which rotated with the cylinder; it was pierced with holes to accommodate the hammer nose, into which the primers might expand, if necessary, without fouling the mechanism. This was reliable, if slow. The earliest cartridges fired lead balls, but later marks were loaded with elongated bullets with hollow, plugged bases to assist expansion into the rifling. This method had been used successfully in the percussion Enfield rifle and its Snider conversion.

Great Britain
## BLAND-PRYSE TYPE REVOLVER

In 1877, Webley began to make a new type of break-open revolver patented by C. Pryse. However, since other makers also appear to have produced similar arms, Webley was clearly not the only patentee. Although the specimen shown here bears no identification marks of any kind, there is every reason to suppose that it is indeed an arm of Bland-Pryse type. The weapon is robustly made: there is a hinge at the bottom front of the frame, and a rear extension of the top frame fits into a corresponding slot in the standing breech, just above the nose of the hammer. There are two vertical, hinged arms behind the cylinder, one on either side of the frame, each with an inward-facing stud on its upper extremity. When the revolver is closed, these studs pass through holes in the breech and engage with recesses on the rear extension, thus holding the arm firmly closed. Pressure on the milled discs at the bottom of the arms disengages the studs and allows the arm to be opened. The latter action also forces out a star-shaped extractor at the rear of the cylinder, throwing out the empty cases.

France
## LE MAT REVOLVER

This revolver is a cartridge version of the earlier percussion Le Mat; it was made in France, probably in about 1868. It is of a somewhat complex, built-up construction, being based on its lower, shot barrel, which is firmly seated in the standing breech and acts also as an axis pin for the revolver cylinder. The lower frame of the upper barrel has a sleeve which fits over the lower barrel; an extension from this is screwed firmly to the lower frame, making what appears to be a good, rigid joint. The upper barrel and cylinder (which has nine chambers) allow the arm to be used as an orthodox single-action cartridge revolver, with a loading gate and a sliding ejector rod of Colt type. In order to load the lower shot barrel, it is necessary first to cock the weapon and then open the side-hinged breechblock by manipulating the catch visible behind the cylinder. The breechblock has its own firing pin; in order to ensure that this is struck, a hinged block on the underside of the hammer is first turned downward. The action of opening the breechblock also activates a semi-circular extractor which engages under the rim of the cartridge case and pushes it clear. This arm is of similar man-stopping type to the others shown here: it was used in French penal colonies in the second half of the 19th century, but it does not appear to have been used for military purposes.

*Like the Webley No 1, the Bland-Pryse was chambered to take the massive ·577in cartridge, which was guaranteed to stop the most determined assailant—dead!*

United States of America
**COLT SINGLE-ACTION ARMY REVOLVER**

| | |
|---|---|
| **Length:** | 11" (279mm) |
| **Weight:** | 35oz (·99kg) |
| **Barrel:** | 5·5" (140mm) |
| **Calibre:** | ·45" (11·4mm) |
| **Rifling:** | 6 groove, r/hand |
| **Capacity:** | Six |
| **Muz Vel:** | c650 f/s (198 m/s) |
| **Sights:** | Fixed |

Belgium
**DOUBLE-BARRELLED REVOLVER**

| | |
|---|---|
| **Length:** | 7·5" (190mm) |
| **Weight:** | 18oz (·51kg) |
| **Barrels:** | 3·75" (95mm) |
| **Calibre:** | ·22" (5·6mm) |
| **Rifling:** | 5 groove, r/hand |
| **Capacity:** | Twelve |
| **Muz Vel:** | c650 f/s (198 m/s) |
| **Sights:** | Fixed |

United States of America
**COLT SINGLE-ACTION ARMY REVOLVER**
The "Artillery" model—so styled from its 5·5in (140mm) barrel—of one of the most famous revolvers of all time. Among other names, it has been called the "New Model Army" and, in the Old West context for which it is best known, the "Frontier" and "Peacemaker"

Belgium
**DOUBLE-BARRELLED REVOLVER**
This is a weapon of good quality but somewhat doubtful utility. Two barrels presumably increase stopping-power significantly, but an orthodox six-chambered revolver in ·32in calibre would be just as efficient, less bulky and easier to handle.

United States of America
**COLT SINGLE-ACTION ARMY REVOLVER**

| | |
|---|---|
| **Length:** | 13" (330mm) |
| **Weight:** | 38oz (1·08kg) |
| **Barrel:** | 7·5" (190mm) |
| **Calibre:** | ·44" (11·2mm) |
| **Rifling:** | 6 groove, r/hand |
| **Capacity:** | Six |
| **Muz Vel:** | c650 f/s (198 m/s) |
| **Sights:** | Fixed |

United States of America
**REMINGTON REVOLVER**

| | |
|---|---|
| **Length:** | 13" (330mm) |
| **Weight:** | 43oz (1·22kg) |
| **Barrel:** | 7·5" (190mm) |
| **Calibre:** | ·44" (11·2mm) |
| **Rifling:** | 6 groove, r/hand |
| **Capacity:** | Six |
| **Muz Vel:** | c700 f/s (213 m/s) |
| **Sights:** | Fixed |

United States of America
**COLT SINGLE-ACTION ARMY REVOLVER**
The "Cavalry" model, with a 7·5in (190mm) barrel, of the famous Colt Single-Action Army series. A Double-Action Army model (see page 77) introduced in 1877 was far less successful than this fine arm, which is still in production in various forms.

United States of America
**REMINGTON REVOLVER**
Although Remington cartridge revolvers like the one seen here were of a quality in keeping with the company's reputation, they could not compete successfully with the well-established weapons made by Colt, and thus were in production only from 1875 until 1894.

United States of America

## COLT SINGLE-ACTION ARMY REVOLVER

This entry should be read in conjunction with that in the third column. Colt's original patent for a mechanically-revolved cylinder expired in 1857—and the rival firm of Smith and Wesson designed a new version by 1856. This was a breechloader, and the fact that Smith and Wesson controlled the Rollin White patent for the bored-through cylinder gave them an original monopoly. The early rimfire cartridges proved reliable and gained wide acceptance. Colt's first venture into this field was to develop a rimless, slightly tapered cartridge which could be loaded into the front face of the cylinder and firmly seated with the orthodox percussion rammer. But this method, known as the Thuer conversion, was only temporary: as soon as possible after the expiry of Smith and Wesson's patent, Colt had a revolver of their own ready to launch on to the market. This arm, which is fully described on the facing page, appeared in 1873 and is sometimes referred to by that date. Colt had gone one step further by designing the new weapon to fire brass-cased centre-fire cartridges with copper caps in their bases. The arm was an immediate success. It was first known as the "New Metallic Cartridge Revolving Pistol", but was later listed under the more familiar title of the Single-Action Army Revolver. The earliest model was of ·45in (11·4mm) calibre and fired a 235-grain (15 gram) lead bullet by means of 617 grains (40 gram) of black powder, but it was later made in a variety of different calibres and in several barrel lengths.

Belgium

## DOUBLE-BARRELLED REVOLVER

One type of double-barrelled revolver, the Le Mat, with barrels of varying calibres, is described on page 59. Another type, with barrels one above the other, allowed the use of two concentric rings of chambers in one large cylinder. But about the most common type is that illustrated here, in which two small-calibre barrels are positioned side-by-side and are fired simultaneously. This weapon is of Belgian make and was probably produced towards the end of the 19th century. The barrels, which are round, appear to have been machined out of a single piece of metal and the top rib then attached. The frame is of bottom-hinged type; the locking device being of the Pryse type, involving the use of two centrally-hinged vertical arms. Each arm has a stud at the top of its inner side; the studs are forced inwards under the pressure of a spring, so that they pass through holes at the top of the standing breech and engage a rearward extension of the top rib. The lock is of double-action type, with a folding trigger which makes the arm convenient for the pocket. The hammer nose is flat and acts on a pair of firing pins mounted in the rear of the standing breech. The fluted cylinder, which is, of necessity, large in relation to the overall dimensions of the weapon, is hollow in the centre to reduce weight. It is fitted with a star-shaped extractor which automatically throws out the rounds or empty cases when the revolver is opened smartly. The butt is of bird-beak type with wooden side plates. The top rib bears the usual Belgian inspection marks.

United States of America

## COLT SINGLE-ACTION ARMY REVOLVER

This famous Colt revolver was available in three barrel lengths: 7·5in (190mm); 5·5in (140mm) and 4·75in (121mm). These were usually referred to as the Cavalry, Artillery and Civilian models respectively; the one illustrated here is the 7·5in (190mm) Cavalry model. Although the arms in the series retained much of their characteristic Colt appearance, there are obvious differences. The frame is solid, with a top strap, the round barrel being screwed into it, and the cylinder is, of course, bored through. The robust, hemispherical standing breech is retained, with a contoured loading gate built into its right side, and ejection is by means of a rod sliding in a sleeve below and to the right of the barrel. The lock is of single-action type. The butt-plates are of walnut on the specimen shown here, but other materials —including hard rubber, ivory and even mother-of-pearl— may be encountered. Production models are usually plainly finished in blue or nickel, but presentation arms may be highly ornate. The arm shown is of ·44in (11·2mm) calibre and is so stamped to the left of the trigger guard. This was a very popular calibre: Winchester's 1873 model rifle was also chambered for the same cartridge, which greatly simplified ammunition supply. A few special models of this revolver with 12in (305mm) barrels were commissioned by a "Western" writer, Ned Buntline, after whom they were named, but these are now rare. This series of revolvers, often known as the "Peacemaker" or "Frontier" models, is still made in various forms.

United States of America

## REMINGTON REVOLVER

The firm of Remington did not begin to make revolvers until 1857 and its earliest products were all pocket pistols. On the outbreak of the American Civil War, large-calibre hand guns of service type were put into production. Expansion continued after the War with the opening up of the West, when the demand, particularly for revolvers, remained high. These revolvers were percussion arms, but the War had seen the rise in popularity of the self-contained metallic cartridge. In the early post-war years, Smith and Wesson had a monopoly in such arms because of their possession of the Rollin White bored-through cylinder patent, but once that had lapsed the field was open. Remington's first cartridge revolver, of 1875, as seen here, differed very little in general appearance from the firm's earlier percussion arm (illustrated on page 29, above). The major mechanical differences are the bored-through cylinder; the loading gate; and the provision of a Colt-type ejector rod working in a sleeve. The distinctively tapered rammer handle of the earlier arm had, of course, become unnecessary; but, as may be seen, it was replaced by a rib of similar dimensions, thus leaving the silhouette unchanged. The trigger-guard of this model is of steel and the butt is fitted with a lanyard ring. The Remingtons were excellent weapons— robust, well-made and accurate. A new version appeared in 1891, but in 1894 Remington reverted to its first interest of long arms, a sphere in which the company still excels, as many modern rifles will bear witness.

United States of America
**SMITH AND WESSON MODEL No 3 REVOLVER**

| | |
|---|---|
| **Length:** | 11·5" (292mm) |
| **Weight:** | 40oz (1·13kg) |
| **Barrel:** | 6" (152mm) |
| **Calibre:** | ·44" (11·2mm) |
| **Rifling:** | 5 groove, r/hand |
| **Capacity:** | Six |
| **Muz Vel:** | c750 f/s (229 m/s) |
| **Sights:** | Fixed |

United States of America
**SMITH AND WESSON ·32 SAFETY, THIRD MODEL**

| | |
|---|---|
| **Length:** | 6·75" (171mm) |
| **Weight:** | 13oz (·37kg) |
| **Barrel:** | 3" (76mm) |
| **Calibre:** | ·32" (8·1mm) |
| **Rifling:** | 5 groove, r/hand |
| **Capacity:** | Six |
| **Muz Vel:** | c800 f/s (244 m/s) |
| **Sights:** | Fixed |

United States of America
**SMITH AND WESSON MODEL No 3 REVOLVER**
This revolver, although never generally popular in the United States, was much favoured by target shooters—and it may be noted that the example illustrated here is fitted with a target sight rather than the round blade usually found on service revolvers.

United States of America
**SMITH AND WESSON ·32 SAFETY, THIRD MODEL**
As an additional safety measure, the hard, black rubber stocks of the revolver are rounded so as to lessen the risk of snagging on the lining of a pocket. Except for the trigger, trigger-guard and catch, this particular example is nickel-plated.

Belgium
**COPY OF SMITH AND WESSON MODEL No 3 REVOLVER**

| | |
|---|---|
| **Length:** | 8" (203mm) |
| **Weight:** | 22oz (·62kg) |
| **Barrel:** | 4" (102mm) |
| **Calibre:** | ·38" (9·6mm) |
| **Rifling:** | 5 groove, l/hand |
| **Capacity:** | Six |
| **Muz Vel:** | c740 f/s (226 m/s) |
| **Sights:** | Fixed |

Belgium
**COPY OF SMITH AND WESSON RUSSIAN MODEL**

| | |
|---|---|
| **Length:** | 12·5" (317mm) |
| **Weight:** | 36oz (1·02kg) |
| **Barrel:** | 8" (203mm) |
| **Calibre:** | ·44" (11·2mm) |
| **Rifling:** | 5 groove, l/hand |
| **Capacity:** | Six |
| **Muz Vel:** | c700 f/s (214 m/s) |
| **Sights:** | Fixed |

Belgium
**COPY OF SMITH AND WESSON MODEL No 3 REVOLVER**
Continental copies of popular American models were very common and there are probably thousands of revolvers like this one still in existence: they sold for a few shillings in the later 19th century.

Belgium
**COPY OF SMITH AND WESSON RUSSIAN MODEL**
The barrel of this continental copy is spuriously inscribed "SMITH AND WESSON", but Belgian proof marks on the cylinder enable its true origin to be established. The butt-plates are of bone or ivory, probably the former, and it is of relatively poor quality.

United States of America
## SMITH AND WESSON MODEL No 3 REVOLVER

Smith and Wesson revolvers of this general type first appeared in 1870, when the company began to make a service-type arm of large calibre, the No 3 First Model American. The arm shown on the colour spread is the New Model No 3. It is chambered to take the ·44in (11·2mm) Russian cartridge. It has a round, tapered barrel with a full top rib, and it is fitted with a target sight instead of the round blade usually found on service models. The revolver is opened by pushing up the milled catch visible in front of the hammer and pushing down the barrel. This automatically forces out the star-shaped ejector, which is mounted on a hexagonal rod and is activated by means of a rack and gear. The six-chambered cylinder is 1·44in (37mm) long: a few later models have cylinders with a length of 1·56in (40mm). The locking device, in itself quite adequate, is further reinforced by the provision of a notch above the hammer nose (visible in the photograph) which engages over a flange on the catch when the hammer is fully down. The lock is of single-action type with a rebounding hammer which, like the trigger and guard, is case-hardened. Although this was a very fine arm and popular with expert target shots, it never really caught on in the United States. American users preferred a more powerful cartridge than was ever considered to be a safe and practical proposition in a break-open arm. Thus, they favoured solid-frame revolvers as a general rule, the only exception being contributed by small, pocket-type arms firing low-powered cartridges.

United States of America
## SMITH AND WESSON ·32 SAFETY, THIRD MODEL

The first Smith and Wesson model with a fully-enclosed hammer appeared on the market in 1888 and was a considerable success; in 1902 it was succeeded by a second model, with relatively minor variations. This, in turn, was replaced by a third model, which remained in production until 1937: the revolver illustrated here is one of the third model weapons. The revolver was made in three barrel lengths, 2in (51mm), 3in (76mm), and 3·5in (89mm): this arm has a 3in (76mm) barrel, which is round with a top rib and a round, blade foresight. The foresight was usually forged integrally with the barrel on the 3in (76mm) and 3·5in (89mm) models; however, in the arm seen here the foresight is inserted into a slot in the rib and pinned. The revolver is opened by pushing up a T-shaped catch with a knurled knob on either side. This allows the barrel to be forced down and brings the automatic extractor into play. Although weapons of this type are often referred to as "hammerless", this is in a sense a misnomer: they have hammers, which are concealed within the frame. They are necessarily, self-cockers only; but this is, of course, no disadvantage in a pocket pistol which was intended to be used for quick shooting at close quarters. It incorporates a safety device in the form of a lever mounted on the back strap. When the butt is properly gripped in preparation for firing, the lever is forced in and allows the lock mechanism to function normally; this makes it an extremely safe weapon.

Belgium

## COPY OF SMITH AND WESSON MODEL No 3 REVOLVER

In 1880 Smith and Wesson introduced a series of double-action, break-open, pocket revolvers in ·38in (9·6mm) calibre. They were useful weapons, for they combined compact dimensions with a cartridge big enough to provide considerable stopping-power; thus, they very soon became popular in the United States and elsewhere. This kind of popularity inevitably led to the pirating of the design, particularly in Belgium, where the revolver seen here originated. The 19th century saw a considerable degree of industrialization in that country: in particular, Belgium's capacity to produce small arms of all kinds increased very rapidly as the century progressed. Although there were large factories, a very considerable part of the Belgian output came from small, anonymous, back-street workshops, usually family concerns. The people employed in such workshops were often skilled as well as hard-working; and although some cheap and unreliable arms were produced, most were adequate—and certainly as good as could be expected at the low price charged. The revolver seen here is a close copy of the Smith and Wesson third model, produced from 1884 until 1895, and is of as good a quality as might reasonably be expected, considering its origins. It has a round barrel with a top rib and a round, brass foresight; the backsight is a notch cut in the front of the barrel catch, which is of the usual T-shape. The lock mechanism is of the orthodox double-action type. The arm has imitation-pearl butt-plates.

Belgium

## COPY OF SMITH AND WESSON RUSSIAN MODEL

In 1871 the firm of Smith and Wesson began to manufacture revolvers for the Russian government, which was then in the process of modernizing its army. The vast orders involved kept the firm going very happily for seven years, although in the long term it led to a huge loss of business in the United States. This was mainly due to the competition of the Colt company, which seized the opportunity offered it to establish almost complete domination of the great markets opened up in the United States by the mass movement of population to the West and Southwest in the decades following the end of the Civil War. Smith and Wesson's Russian models were fine weapons of their type, and thus they were inevitably copied. European countries, and Belgium in particular, were quick to turn out their own versions of any popular arm. These were usually made in small, family workshops, where they could be produced a good deal more cheaply than their more reputable prototypes. Of course, the copies were of varying quality: at best, they never attained the quality of the originals; at worst, they were positively dangerous. The revolver illustrated here, which is based on the various Smith and Wesson Russian models, is of relatively poor quality. The workmanship and general finish are crude. In particular, it lacks the groove across the top of the hammer which engages a flange on the barrel catch—which is a feature always to be found on the genuine article. The lock is of double-action type; it does not rebound, but is fitted with a manual half-cock.

Austria
**RAST AND GASSER MODEL 1898**

| | |
|---|---|
| **Length:** | 8·75" (222mm) |
| **Weight:** | 34oz (·96kg) |
| **Barrel:** | 4·5" (114mm) |
| **Calibre:** | ·31" (8mm) |
| **Rifling:** | 4 groove, r/hand |
| **Capacity:** | Eight |
| **Muz Vel:** | c700 f/s (213 m/s) |
| **Sights:** | Fixed |

Italy
**BODEO MODEL 1889 SERVICE REVOLVER**

| | |
|---|---|
| **Length:** | 10·5" (267mm) |
| **Weight:** | 32oz (·91kg) |
| **Barrel:** | 4·5" (114mm) |
| **Calibre:** | ·41" (10·4mm) |
| **Rifling:** | 4 groove, r/hand |
| **Capacity:** | Six |
| **Muz Vel:** | c650 f/s (198 m/s) |
| **Sights:** | Fixed |

Austria
**RAST AND GASSER MODEL 1898**
Although oddly-shaped by modern standards, this is a sound, well-made revolver. In 1898 it was adopted for the use of infantry officers and non-commissioned officers of the Austrian Army.

Italy
**BODEO MODEL 1889 SERVICE REVOLVER**
This Italian service revolver was also made in a round-barrelled version, with a trigger-guard. It remained in service with the Italian Army from its adoption in 1891 almost until World War II.

Japan
**MEIJI TYPE 26 SERVICE REVOLVER**

| | |
|---|---|
| **Length:** | 9·25" (235mm) |
| **Weight:** | 32oz (·91kg) |
| **Barrel:** | 4·7" (119mm) |
| **Calibre:** | ·35" (9mm) |
| **Rifling:** | 4 groove, r/hand |
| **Capacity:** | Six |
| **Muz Vel:** | c600 f/s (183 m/s) |
| **Sights:** | Fixed |

Belgium
**GALAND VELO-DOG REVOLVER**

| | |
|---|---|
| **Length:** | 4·7" (119mm) |
| **Weight:** | 10·5oz (·30kg) |
| **Barrel:** | 1·2" (30mm) |
| **Calibre:** | ·216" (5·5mm) |
| **Rifling:** | 4 groove, r/hand |
| **Capacity:** | Six |
| **Muz Vel:** | c400 f/s (122 m/s) |
| **Sights:** | Fixed |

Japan
**MEIJI TYPE 26 SERVICE REVOLVER**
It is not surprising that there is little that is original in the design of this revolver, for it was produced at a time when Japan was only just emerging from some three centuries of seclusion.

Belgium
**GALAND VELO-DOG REVOLVER**
Revolvers like the one seen here were designed principally for the use of pioneer cyclists of the later 19th century—who appear to have been much troubled by fierce dogs! Although non-lethal cartridges loaded with salt, pepper or dust-shot might be used, it seems an extreme way of dealing with a temporary nuisance.

Austria

## RAST AND GASSER MODEL 1898

This Austrian Service revolver of 1898 may have been the last to bear the name of Leopold Gasser, whose Austrian factories produced revolvers on a large scale during the last quarter of the 19th century. They were used by many Balkan armies. It is of solid-frame type, with a round barrel screwed in; its eight-chambered cylinder is plain, except for slots for the stop. The revolver is loaded through a bottom-hinged loading gate, the inside of which is fitted with a small projection which engages the frame and prevents it from being drawn farther back than the horizontal. When the loading gate is open, the hammer is disconnected, but the cylinder may still be rotated by the action of the trigger, which speeds up loading. The usual groove is provided on the frame to ensure that the cartridges are not obstructed on their way in. The ejector rod is hollow and works over a rod which is connected to the projection below the barrel; this projection also houses the front end of the axis pin. When it is not in use, the handle of the ejector rod fits round the axis pin. The lock is of double action type and there is a separate firing-pin on the frame. Access to the mechanism is by means of a hinged cover which extends over almost the entire left side of the frame (the rear hinge is visible, just above the butt). The revolver is of old-fashioned appearance and it is best fired with the arm slightly bent; it is, however, very well made, although the cartridge it fired was too lacking in power to be of very much use for service purposes.

Italy

## BODEO MODEL 1889 SERVICE REVOLVER

The Bodeo revolver took its name from the head of the Italian commission which recommended its adoption in 1889. This recommendation being approved, the Bodeo was put into production; by 1891 it had become the standard Italian service revolver, remaining in service for at least 50 years. The Model 1889 was made in two distinct types: a round-barrelled version, with a trigger-guard; and an octagonal-barrelled version, with a folding trigger. The revolver seen here is of the latter type. Although not an arm of particular distinction, the Bodeo was simple and robust—which is presumably why it lasted so long. The barrel is screwed into the frame, and the cylinder is loaded through a bottom-hinged gate which is drawn backwards to open it. Ejection is by means of a rod which is normally housed in the hollow axis pin. As in the Rast-Gasser revolver, illustrated above it, the loading gate was connected to the hammer in such a way that, when it was opened, the hammer would not function, although the action of the trigger still turned the cylinder. This arrangement, which is known as the "Abadie" system, is frequently found on continental weapons. Revolvers of this type were made in a variety of Italian factories, and during World War I a number were also manufactured in Spain for use by the Italian Army. It was officially superseded by a self-loading pistol quite early in the 20th century, but many remained in service—and in sporadic production at both Italian and Spanish factories—up to World War II.

Japan
## MEIJI TYPE 26 SERVICE REVOLVER

Many Japanese arms, including the revolver seen here, were dated from the accession of the reigning Emperor. This arm was made in 1893, which was the 26th year of the Meiji Era, and it is therefore known as the Type 26 revolver. There is little that is original about this weapon. It is, in fact, a quite remarkably composite arm, incorporating a variety of ideas derived from a careful study of Western weapons. The Imperial Japanese Navy had earlier purchased a quantity of Smith and Wesson No 3 Models; these had been found satisfactory, so it is perhaps natural that the American arm should have formed a basis for this one. In addition, however, there are elements derived from the arms of Galand, Nagant and others. It has an octagonal barrel with a foresight bed into which a sight is pinned; the backsight is incorporated with the top frame. The weapon is opened by lifting the top catch, after which the barrel can be forced down to bring the automatic ejector into action. The lock is of self-cocking variety and, as the mechanism is sluggish, this makes accurate shooting almost impossible. In view of the fairly primitive state of Japanese industry at the time that this arm was produced, it is not surprising that it is generally of poor material and finish. It was issued quite extensively as a cavalry arm, but its trigger-pull must have made it very ineffective except at point-blank range. It was officially superseded by a self-loading pistol before World War II, but thousands of Type 26 revolvers appear to have remained in service.

Belgium
## GALAND VELO-DOG REVOLVER

As with many other weapons, the term "Velo-Dog" is used to describe a fairly clearly defined group of weapons, rather than one particular arm. Most weapons of this type were cheap pocket revolvers, and they were made in very considerable numbers at the end of the 19th century. They were essentially a continental product, being made in quantity in Belgium, France, Germany, Italy and Spain; the last-named country was particularly prolific. The Velo-Dog was invented by Charles François Galand, whose name has been mentioned earlier in connection with self-extracting revolvers. Galand's first model was of open-frame type, with an orthodox trigger and guard, as on the arm seen here; but later models, wherever produced, tended to have solid frames, completely enclosed hammers and folding triggers. The revolver illustrated is, therefore, a relatively minority type. The earliest Velo-Dogs fired a long 5·5mm cartridge with a light bullet; later they were designed to fire ·22" (5·6mm), 6mm and 8mm Lebel rimmed cartridges, and even 6·35mm and 7·65mm rimless rounds. According to Hogg and Weeks in *Pistols of the World,* the name was derived from "Velocipede" (the early term for a bicycle) and "Dog", although in view of the arm's geographical origins this seems to be an odd linguistic mixture. There is, however, little doubt that these revolvers were designed principally for use by pioneer cyclists when troubled by dogs. Arms of this type were still advertised in continental makers' catalogues after World War I.

Great Britain
**ENFIELD MARK II SERVICE REVOLVER**

| | |
|---|---|
| **Length:** | 11·5" (292mm) |
| **Weight:** | 40oz (1·13kg) |
| **Barrel:** | 5·75" (146mm) |
| **Calibre:** | ·476" (12·1mm) |
| **Rifling:** | 7 groove, r/hand |
| **Capacity:** | Six |
| **Muz Vel:** | c700 f/s (213 m/s) |
| **Sights:** | Fixed |

Great Britain
**WEBLEY R.I.C. REVOLVER No 2**

| | |
|---|---|
| **Length:** | 8·25" (210mm) |
| **Weight:** | 27oz (·76kg) |
| **Barrel:** | 3·5" (89mm) |
| **Calibre:** | ·45" (11·4mm) |
| **Rifling:** | 5 groove, r/hand |
| **Capacity:** | Six |
| **Muz Vel:** | c650 f/s (198 m/s) |
| **Sights:** | Fixed |

Great Britain
**ENFIELD MARK II SERVICE REVOLVER**
Note the spring catch just in front of the hammer, where the barrel is hinged to the front of the frame. It was thought that a top-break arm of Webley type could not safely handle the ·476in round.

Great Britain
**WEBLEY R.I.C. REVOLVER No 2**
This particular example (which has the serial number 10974) of one of the most famous British revolvers was carried by Major Webb of the Bengal Cavalry during the Second Afghan War of 1878-1888.

Great Britain
**WEBLEY R.I.C. REVOLVER No 1**

| | |
|---|---|
| **Length:** | 9·25" (235mm) |
| **Weight:** | 30oz (·85kg) |
| **Barrel:** | 4·5" (114mm) |
| **Calibre:** | ·45" (11·4mm) |
| **Rifling:** | 5 groove, r/hand |
| **Capacity:** | Six |
| **Muz Vel:** | c650 f/s (198 m/s) |
| **Sights:** | Fixed |

Italy
**CHAMELOT-DELVIGNE ITALIAN SERVICE REVOLVER**

| | |
|---|---|
| **Length:** | 11·2" (284mm) |
| **Weight:** | 40oz (1·13kg) |
| **Barrel:** | 6·25" (159mm) |
| **Calibre:** | ·41" (10·4mm) |
| **Rifling:** | 5 groove, r/hand |
| **Capacity:** | Six |
| **Muz Vel:** | c625 f/s (190 m/s) |
| **Sights:** | Fixed |

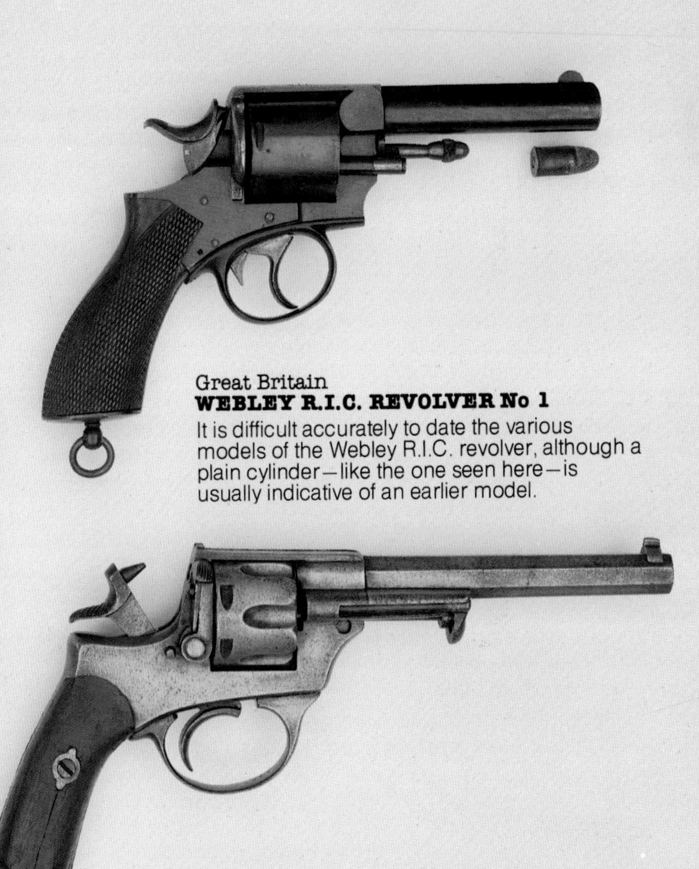

Great Britain
**WEBLEY R.I.C. REVOLVER No 1**
It is difficult accurately to date the various models of the Webley R.I.C. revolver, although a plain cylinder—like the one seen here—is usually indicative of an earlier model.

Italy
**CHAMELOT-DELVIGNE ITALIAN SERVICE REVOLVER**
Chamelot-Delvigne service revolvers were made in several Italian factories: on the left side of the frame of this example is the name of the Royal Manufactory of Glisenti, Brescia.

Great Britain
## ENFIELD MARK II SERVICE REVOLVER

Colonial campaigns showed that the bullet of the standard Adams ·45in revolver could not always be relied upon to stop a charging fanatic, so in the late 1870s the British government decided upon a new and more powerful round of ·476in calibre—and a new arm to fire it. Designed by Owen Jones, it was approved for service in 1880. (The specimen on the colour spread is a Mark II.) As may be seen, the barrel is hinged to the front of the frame and fastened with a spring catch just in front of the hammer. However, when the revolver is opened and the barrel forced downward, the cylinder remains in the same axis and is simply drawn forward along its pin. This leaves the cases held by their rims in a star-shaped extractor on the standing breech, whence they can be shaken clear. The need for the cylinder to be drawn well forward accounts for the rather ugly bulge below the barrel. The Enfield Mark II was adopted in 1882. Its main points of difference from the Mark I are the provision of a device in the loading gate which prevents the action from working if the gate is open, and vice-versa, and the fitting of a safety catch on the left side of the frame.

*When the Enfield Mk I is opened the cylinder is drawn forward. Note the star-shaped extractor.*

Great Britain
## WEBLEY R.I.C. REVOLVER No 2

The first revolvers of this type were manufactured by P. Webley and Son of Birmingham in 1867. They immediately became popular as robust and reliable service weapons; they were probably the best-known of Webley products and made the firm famous. It is a measure of their quality that they remained in production for more than 30 years. In 1868, to police a troubled land, the Royal Irish Constabulary was raised as a paramilitary body armed with rifles, carbines or revolvers—the Webley being the first adopted and thus being known thereafter as the Royal Irish Constabulary revolver. The specimen illustrated here is the No 2 Model and was probably made in about 1876. The barrel is round, although the shape of the top rib gives a distinct impression of taper, and is screwed into the frame. It has a semi-round foresight, slotted in; the backsight is a long, V-shaped groove along the top strap. The six-chambered cylinder is plain except for raised flanges at the rear; the ends of these are held by the cylinder stop, which rises from the lower frame when the trigger is pressed. The extractor pin is housed in the hollow cylinder axis pin when it is not in use, but it can be withdrawn on a swivel in order to align it with the appropriate chamber. Once the pin is drawn, the cylinder may be removed by drawing the axis pin forward by means of its flat, milled head. Access to the chambers is by means of a loading gate which is hinged at the bottom and opens sideways against a flat spring. The lock is of double-action type.

Great Britain

## WEBLEY R.I.C. REVOLVER No 1

The arm illustrated here is the Royal Irish Constabulary No 1 Model; but as the manufacture of all varieties of this revolver seems to have overlapped a good deal, it is not possible to date it very accurately. It has a basically round barrel which is, however, slightly raised on its upper side, on which a flat rib has been machined. The foresight is slotted in, and the backsight, as usual, consists of a long groove on the top strap. The barrel is screwed into a solid frame. The six-chambered cylinder is plain, except for recesses for the cylinder stop at the rear end. Plain cylinders, it should be noted, are usually inidicative of earlier models: on later models the cylinders are fluted to achieve a small reduction in weight. The extractor is of the usual type, although its knob is acorn-shaped. The loading gate is standard. The revolver has a double-action lock, with a half-cock which holds the nose of the hammer well clear of the cartridges in the chambers. The chequered walnut butt is of one-piece type and is held by two vertical screws; one downward from the back of the frame and one upward from the butt-cap. These revolvers were made in a variety of calibres, none smaller than ·410in (10·4mm), and they were widely used all over the British Empire. They were also very extensively copied in various European countries. Among notable R.I.C. models was the ·442in Model 1872, with a 2·5in barrel. Although somewhat bulky for the purpose, this was a pocket model which set a trend to be followed by a wide range of short-barrelled Webley arms.

Italy

## CHAMELOT-DELVIGNE ITALIAN SERVICE REVOLVER

The robust Chamelot-Delvigne double-action lock, first manufactured by Pirlot Frères of Liège, Belgium, very quickly became widely used in Europe after 1870 because of its simplicity and reliability. It was adopted for service weapons by France, Belgium, Switzerland and Italy, among others. The revolver seen here is the Italian version of the Chamelot-Delvigne et Schmidt Model 1872 (Schmidt was a Swiss officer who made some changes in design). There was also a version with a folding trigger—and, therefore, of course, no trigger-guard. The arm is of solid-frame type, with an octagonal barrel which is screwed into the main frame. The foresight is slotted in and the backsight is a U-notch on the lump (visible just in front of the hammer), the top strap also being grooved. The six-chambered cylinder is grooved and has rear notches for the cylinder stop. The ejector rod works in a sleeve; when it is not in use, its head is turned in under the barrel, where it fits over the front end of the cylinder axis pin. In order to remove the cylinder, it is first necessary to turn down the head of the ejector rod and press in a stud on the left front of the frame; this allows the pin to be drawn forward. The spring loading gate is hinged at the bottom and is opened by drawing it to the rear. There is a small stop on the frame, against which the gate rests when in the open position. The lock is of double-action type; very slight pressure on the trigger lifts the hammer to the half-cock position, which allows the cylinder to be rotated for loading.

Great Britain
## TRANTER "ARMY" REVOLVER

| | |
|---|---|
| **Length:** | 11·75" (298mm) |
| **Weight:** | 36oz (1·02kg) |
| **Barrel:** | 6" (152mm) |
| **Calibre:** | ·45" (11·4mm) |
| **Rifling:** | 7 groove, r/hand |
| **Capacity:** | Six |
| **Muz Vel:** | c650 f/s (198 m/s) |
| **Sights:** | Fixed |

Great Britain
## WEBLEY NEW MODEL ARMY EXPRESS

| | |
|---|---|
| **Length:** | 10·5" (267mm) |
| **Weight:** | 38oz (1·08kg) |
| **Barrel:** | 5·5" (140mm) |
| **Calibre:** | ·45" (11·4mm) |
| **Rifling:** | 7 groove, r/hand |
| **Capacity:** | Six |
| **Muz Vel:** | c700 f/s (213 m/s) |
| **Sights:** | Fixed |

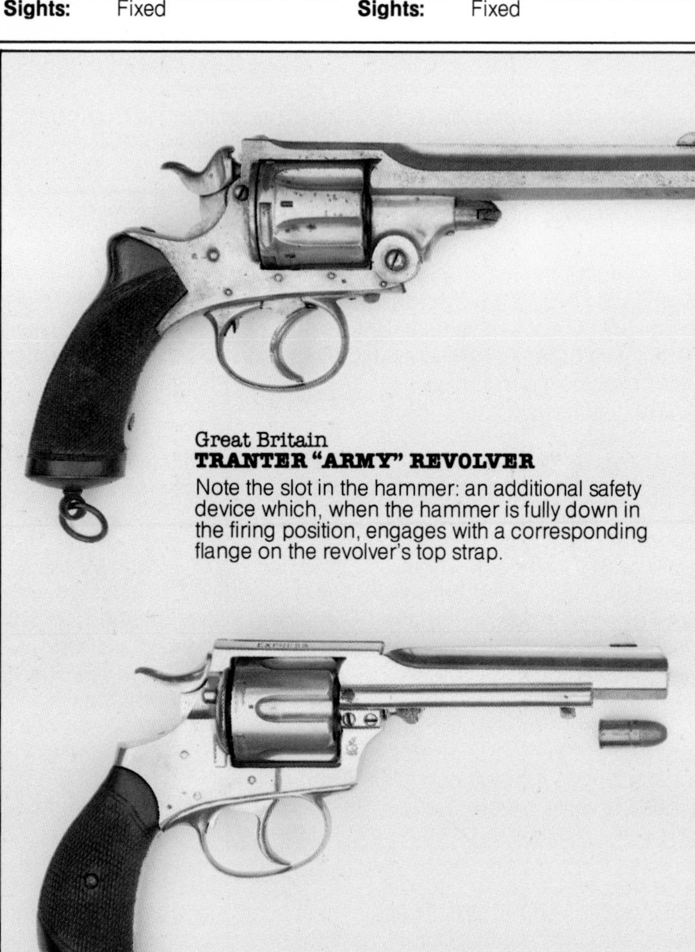

Great Britain
**TRANTER "ARMY" REVOLVER**
Note the slot in the hammer: an additional safety device which, when the hammer is fully down in the firing position, engages with a corresponding flange on the revolver's top strap.

Great Britain
**WEBLEY NEW MODEL ARMY EXPRESS**
Unlike its American rival (see facing page, top), this Webley was acknowledged to be a robust and reliable arm. Note the famous "winged bullet" trademark on the right side of the frame.

United States of America
**COLT DOUBLE-ACTION ARMY REVOLVER**

| | |
|---|---|
| **Length:** | 10·25" (260mm) |
| **Weight:** | 36oz (1·02kg) |
| **Barrel:** | 5·5" (140mm) |
| **Calibre:** | ·476" (12·1mm) |
| **Rifling:** | 6 groove, r/hand |
| **Capacity:** | Six |
| **Muz Vel:** | c750 f/s (229 m/s) |
| **Sights:** | Fixed |

United States of America
**SMITH AND WESSON HAND EJECTOR REVOLVER**

| | |
|---|---|
| **Length:** | 11·75" (298mm) |
| **Weight:** | 38oz (1·08kg) |
| **Barrel:** | 6·5" (165mm) |
| **Calibre:** | ·455" (11·5mm) |
| **Rifling:** | 6 groove, r/hand |
| **Capacity:** | Six |
| **Muz Vel:** | c650 f/s (198 m/s) |
| **Sights:** | Fixed |

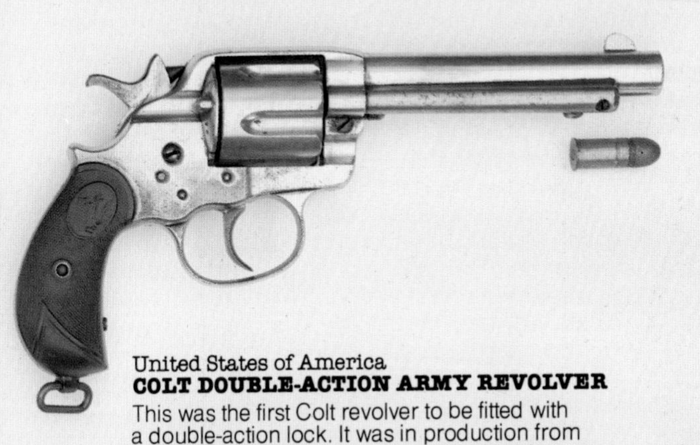

United States of America
**COLT DOUBLE-ACTION ARMY REVOLVER**
This was the first Colt revolver to be fitted with a double-action lock. It was in production from 1877 until 1909, but never became popular: users alleged that it was poorly balanced and unreliable.

United States of America
**SMITH AND WESSON HAND EJECTOR REVOLVER**
A beautiful weapon in mint condition: this is the special version of the Smith and Wesson Hand Ejector revolver made for the British Army and chambered for the ·455in (11·5mm) cartridge.

Great Britain

## TRANTER "ARMY" REVOLVER

William Tranter (whose double-trigger revolvers are shown on pages 36-37) quickly saw the advantages of hinged-frame or break-open revolvers, and by 1879 had put his arm of this type into production. It has an octagonal barrel with a raised top rib and a round fore-sight (the backsight being a groove on the back end of the top strap), and a six-chambered fluted cylinder with an automatic ejector. The cylinder may be removed by first opening the revolver and then pressing the milled catch visible below the barrel; the cylinder may then be lifted off its axis pin. The lock is of double-action type and has a rebounding hammer. The locking system consists of a rear extension to the top strap, with a rectangular aperture which fits over a shaped projection on top of the standing breech. The long, pivoted hook on the left of the frame is basically similar to that on the Webley, but fits over a projection on the top frame. An additional safety device is provided by a slot in the hammer (clearly visible in the photograph) which, when the hammer is fully down in the firing position, engages a corresponding flange on the revolver's strap.

*Tranter's "Army" revolver was in British service use from the late 1870s until 1887.*

Great Britain

## WEBLEY NEW MODEL ARMY EXPRESS

The appearance in 1877 of the new Colt double-action revolver (illustrated on the previous page, above) was quickly followed by that of a new Webley revolver of very similar appearance. Like the Colt, the Webley is a solid-frame revolver, with a loading gate and a sliding ejector rod. Its barrel, which is basically octagonal but with a higher and narrower top flat, is screwed into the frame, although the joint is virtually imperceptible. It has an unusually large trigger-guard, presumably so that it may be used by a man wearing gloves. Its bird-beak butt is somewhat larger than that of the corresponding Colt, and is a good deal more comfortable to handle as a result. The arm was made in one calibre only, nominally ·45in (11·4mm), but, like all Webley service arms of the period, it would accept cartridges of both ·455in (11·5mm) and ·476in (12·1mm) calibre. There was only one standard length of barrel—5·5in (140mm), as seen here—but a few models were made with 12in (305mm) barrels to special orders, and these were supplied with a detachable shoulder stock. In spite of its strong similarity to the new Colt it is, in fact, probable (according to *The Webley Story* by Dowell) that it was based on a prototype designed some ten years earlier to handle the heavy ·577in (14·6mm) pistol cartridge used in the Webley No 1 (illustrated on page 56); for it does not seem possible that a completely new arm could have been put into production in the time which elapsed between the appearance of the new Colt and that of the Webley.

United States of America

## COLT DOUBLE-ACTION ARMY REVOLVER

In 1877 the Colt company added a new revolver to its existing range: the Double-Action Army model, illustrated here. It has the usual solid frame, with a round barrel screwed into it and an ejector rod sliding in a sleeve. The six-chambered cylinder has a loading gate, and a cartridge groove is provided on the right-hand side of the frame. The butt is of the type known as bird-beak and has a swivel for a strap or a flat lanyard. This is the first Colt revolver to have been fitted with a double-action lock in place of the popular and well-tried single-action mechanism. It is possible that the United States Cavalry may have expressed a preference for such a weapon, which was faster to operate in a mêlée. The revolver was made in three major calibres—·32in (8·1mm); ·38in (9·6mm); and ·45in (11·4mm)—and in three barrel lengths: 4·75in (121mm); 5·5in (140mm); and 7·5in (190mm). The calibre of the revolver illustrated here is, however, ·476in (12·1mm), which indicates that this particular specimen was probably made for the British market—for this was the standard British service calibre at the time. This attribution is confirmed by the fact that the words "DEPOT 14 PALL MALL LONDON" have been added to the standard inscription on the barrel. This model continued to be made in the United States until 1909, but it never proved popular: it had the reputation of being both badly balanced and mechanically unreliable—remarkable and almost unprecedented allegations to be made against a Colt product.

United States of America

## SMITH AND WESSON HAND EJECTOR REVOLVER

The Smith and Wesson No 3 revolver (page 64, top), never really became popular in the United States, where there was inherent distrust of the hinged-frame revolver when used with the powerful cartridges which were then popular. Thus, by the end of the 19th century, Smith and Wesson had produced a solid-frame revolver. The principle is simple and reliable: pushing forward a milled catch on the left of the frame allows the cylinder to be swung out to the left on a separate yoke. Then the extractor is manually operated by means of the pin, a method which is only marginally slower than a hinged-frame type. The version seen here first appeared in 1908 and was variously known as the "·44 Hand Ejector First Model"; the "New Century"; the "Gold Seal"; or the "Triple Lock". The latter name came from the fact that the cylinder locked not only at the rear, but also by means of one bolt into the front end of the rod and a second which emerged from the casing below it. The lock is of rebounding, double action type and, as with all Smith and Wesson arms, works very smoothly. The standard calibre for production arms was ·44in (11·2mm), and it was chambered for the special cartridge, but arms in various other calibres were also made. A small number of original ·44in (11·2mm) calibre revolvers were converted to fire the British ·455in (11·5mm) Eley cartridge, mostly at the outbreak of World War I, but later a special version was made and sold to the British Army in some quantity. The specimen shown is one of the latter arms.

Great Britain
### WEBLEY-FOSBERY SELF-COCKING REVOLVER

| | |
|---|---|
| **Length:** | 11·5" (292mm) |
| **Weight:** | 38oz (1·08kg) |
| **Barrel:** | 7·5" (190mm) |
| **Calibre:** | ·455" (11·5mm) |
| **Rifling:** | 7 groove, r/hand |
| **Capacity:** | Six |
| **Muz Vel:** | c650 f/s (198 m/s) |
| **Sights:** | Fixed |

Great Britain
### WEBLEY AND SCOTT Mk VI (·22in) REVOLVER

| | |
|---|---|
| **Length:** | 11" (279mm) |
| **Weight:** | 38oz (1·08kg) |
| **Barrel:** | 6" (152mm) |
| **Calibre:** | ·22" (5·6mm) |
| **Rifling:** | 7 groove, r/hand |
| **Capacity:** | Six |
| **Muz Vel:** | c600 f/s (183 m/s) |
| **Sights:** | Fixed |

Great Britain
**WEBLEY-FOSBERY SELF-COCKING REVOLVER**
The speed and accuracy of the Webley-Fosbery were proved when Walter Winans, a famous pistol shot, used it to put six shots into a 2in (51mm) bull from 12 paces in seven seconds. Even so, it did not become popular among less expert users.

Great Britain
**WEBLEY AND SCOTT Mk VI (·22in) REVOLVER**
In service calibre this was a solid and reliable arm, well suited to trench warfare. A bayonet was developed to make it even more effective at close quarters, but was not officially issued.

Great Britain
**WEBLEY AND SCOTT Mk V REVOLVER**

| | |
|---|---|
| **Length:** | 11" (279mm) |
| **Weight:** | 38oz (1·08kg) |
| **Barrel:** | 6" (152mm) |
| **Calibre:** | ·455" (11·5mm) |
| **Rifling:** | 7 groove, r/hand |
| **Capacity:** | Six |
| **Muz Vel:** | c650 f/s (198 m/s) |
| **Sights:** | Fixed |

Great Britain
**KYNOCH REVOLVER**

| | |
|---|---|
| **Length:** | 11·5" (292mm) |
| **Weight:** | 42oz (1·19kg) |
| **Barrel:** | 6" (152mm) |
| **Calibre:** | ·455" (11·5mm) |
| **Rifling:** | 7 groove, r/hand |
| **Capacity:** | Six |
| **Muz Vel:** | c650 f/s (198 m/s) |
| **Sights:** | Fixed |

Great Britain
**WEBLEY AND SCOTT Mk V REVOLVER**
This is almost certainly the rarest of the Webley and Scott government series: it was sealed as the standard government pistol in December 1913, but superseded in 1915 after only 20,000 had been made.

Great Britain
**KYNOCH REVOLVER**
The lock of the Kynoch revolver is closely based on that originally invented by William Tranter. Compare this double-trigger revolver with the Tranter arms illustrated on pages 36-37.

Great Britain

## WEBLEY-FOSBERY SELF-COCKING REVOLVER

Colonel George Vincent Fosbery, V.C., retired from the British Army in 1877 and devoted his talents to the development of an efficient machine gun. By the end of the 19th century he had also invented a unique revolver, seen here, which made use of recoil to rotate the cylinder and cock the hammer. This revolver, which was made by Webley and Scott, was first demonstrated at Bisley in 1900 and was put into production the following year. It was of service calibre and handled and loaded in exactly the same way as the standard issue revolver—but with the very important difference that after the first shot the recoil did much of the work: all the firer needed to do was apply light pressure to the trigger, a fact which made for both speed and accuracy. As will be clear from the photograph, the barrel and cylinder were made in such a way that they were free to recoil along guide ribs on the butt and trigger component. On the way back, the cylinder was rotated one-twelfth by the action of a stud working in the zig-zag grooves on its surface, also cocking the action; going forward, the cylinder turned a further one-twelfth, bringing the next chamber into line with the hammer. The revolver was fast and accurate, but was not a popular service weapon: mud and dirt tended to clog the recoiling apparatus, which naturally had to be made to fine tolerances; and also, unless the weapon was fired with an absolutely rigid arm, the recoil was not always sufficient to ensure smooth working.

Great Britain

## WEBLEY AND SCOTT Mk VI (·22in) REVOLVER

In 1915 there appeared the Webley and Scott Mark VI revolver, perhaps the best known of all British service pistols. It did not vary very much from its predecessors, except that the bird-beak butt of the earlier models was replaced by a standard type with a straight lower edge. This weapon was made in large numbers, Webley having a contract to deliver 2,500 weekly. To give intended users some preliminary practice, a small-calibre version (illustrated here) was made. It fired ·22in (5·6mm) rimfire cartridges, allowing the revolver to be used on indoor ranges, and was economical in ammunition. As may be seen, it bears a strong resemblance to its parent arm (illustrated on page 85, top). The main differences are its round barrel and its stepped cylinder, but its locking system, trigger-pull and method of ejection resemble the orthodox Mark VI. There is a slightly different version, which is sometimes fitted with a shorter cylinder, the barrel then being correspondingly extended to the rear. It is a very accurate and well-balanced weapon and proved to be suitable for introductory practice for beginners; but it was not of much instructional value otherwise, because of the complete absence of recoil. And recoil, which tends to throw the muzzle more or less violently upward, is the chief difficulty for the novice user to overcome when using full-bore ammunition. In service calibre, the Webley and Scott Mark VI remained the standard pistol of the British Army until replaced by an Enfield ·38in in the 1930s.

Great Britain

## WEBLEY AND SCOTT Mk V REVOLVER

The first of the Webley series of government service revolvers, the Mark I, adopted 1887, was replaced in 1894 by a Mark II. This, in its turn, gave place in 1897 to a Mark III, which was chambered to take cartridges of ·45in (11·4mm), ·455in (11·5mm) and ·476in (12·1mm) and had a different system of releasing the cylinder. The Mark IV which followed came into service in 1899; it is very often referred to as the Boer War model, for it was extensively used there.

In December 1913, the Mark V was sealed as the standard government pistol, but only 20,000 were made before it was superseded in 1915 by the Mark VI (illustrated on page 85, top). Thus, the Mark V is almost certainly the rarest of all the Webley and Scott government series. In general appearance it resembles its predecessors. It has an octagonal barrel with an integral foresight bed, the blade being inserted separately and held in place by a small screw. The locking system remains unchanged from earlier marks, as do the general details of the lock mechanism. The new system of removing the cylinder, first used on the Mark III, was retained. It consists of a cam (visible below the holster guide), which engages a slot in the front of the cylinder. Loosening the screw allows it to be pushed downwards: the cylinder may then be lifted clear. The butt is of the familiar bird-beak type, and this was the last mark to feature it. Most Mark Vs had 4in (102mm) barrels, but a few —the revolver seen here among them—had barrels that were 2in (51mm) longer.

Great Britain

## KYNOCH REVOLVER

In 1880 the British Government adopted the Enfield revolver (page 72, top). Further trials, and combat use, showed that the Enfield was not good enough, and a number of makers began to develop models they hoped might replace it. One such arm was the Kynoch revolver, illustrated here. It appears to have been originally patented by a British inventor named H. Schlund in 1885 and 1886, and it was subsequently manufactured in a wide variety of calibres by George Kynoch in his gun factory at Aston Cross, Birmingham. The Kynoch revolver illustrated here is a heavy arm of service calibre: it is, in fact, of the type which the maker presumably hoped would be at least in contention as a replacement for the unpopular Enfield. It has an octagonal barrel with a top rib and an integral, half-round foresight. It is of hinged-frame construction, and is opened by pushing forward the catch which can be seen at the rear of the frame. When the weapon is opened thus, the automatic extractor is brought into play. By far the most interesting aspect of the arm, however, is its lock, which is based closely on the type originally invented by William Tranter (illustrated on pages 36 and 37). Pressure on the lower trigger—which is, in effect, a cocking lever—brings the concealed hammer to full-cock; subsequently, a very light touch on the trigger is sufficient to fire it. A later Kynoch version was made with a much shorter double-trigger, entirely contained within the trigger-guard, but the type never achieved much popularity.

United States of America
**COLT OFFICIAL POLICE REVOLVER**

| | |
|---|---|
| **Length:** | 10·25" (260mm) |
| **Weight:** | 34oz (·96kg) |
| **Barrel:** | 5" (127mm) |
| **Calibre:** | ·38" (9·6mm) |
| **Rifling:** | 6 groove, l/hand |
| **Capacity:** | Six |
| **Muz Vel:** | c700 f/s (213 m/s) |
| **Sights:** | Fixed |

United States of America
**SMITH AND WESSON MILITARY AND POLICE 1ST MOD.**

| | |
|---|---|
| **Length:** | 8" (203mm) |
| **Weight:** | 28oz (·79kg) |
| **Barrel:** | 3·25" (83mm) |
| **Calibre:** | ·38" (9·6mm) |
| **Rifling:** | 7 groove, r/hand |
| **Capacity:** | Six |
| **Muz Vel:** | c600 f/s (183 m/s) |
| **Sights:** | Fixed |

United States of America
**COLT OFFICIAL POLICE REVOLVER**
This is one of the many Colt Official Police revolvers supplied to the British Army during World War II. Note the famous "rearing horse" trademark in the white metal medallion on the butt-plate.

United States of America
**SMITH AND WESSON MILITARY AND POLICE 1ST MOD.**
The barrel of this revolver, originally 5in (127mm) long, has been cut down to 3·25in (83mm), and a ramp foresight added. The work has been fairly well done and is difficult to detect immediately.

Great Britain
**WEBLEY AND SCOTT Mk VI REVOLVER**

| | |
|---|---|
| **Length:** | 11" (279mm) |
| **Weight:** | 37oz (1·05kg) |
| **Barrel:** | 6" (152mm) |
| **Calibre:** | ·455" (11·5mm) |
| **Rifling:** | 7 groove, r/hand |
| **Capacity:** | Six |
| **Muz Vel:** | c650 f/s (198 m/s) |
| **Sights:** | Fixed |

United States of America
**MERIDEN POCKET REVOLVER**

| | |
|---|---|
| **Length:** | 6·5" (165mm) |
| **Weight:** | 14oz (·4kg) |
| **Barrel:** | 3" (76mm) |
| **Calibre:** | ·32" (8·1mm) |
| **Rifling:** | 5 groove, r/hand |
| **Capacity:** | Five |
| **Muz Vel:** | c550 f/s (168 m/s) |
| **Sights:** | Fixed |

Great Britain
**WEBLEY AND SCOTT Mk VI REVOLVER**
This excellent revolver was made in huge quantity and, despite being superseded after World War I by the Webley ·38in Mark IV, was still carried by many British Army officers in World War II.

United States of America
**MERIDEN POCKET REVOLVER**
The manufacturer of this rather shoddy arm was one of the many similar companies in the USA in the later 19th century, when cartridge revolvers had become popular and industrial methods were sufficiently advanced to turn them out quickly and cheaply.

United States of America
## COLT OFFICIAL POLICE REVOLVER

This revolver had its origins in the Colt New Navy model, which first appeared in 1889 and was adopted by the United States Navy in 1892. This was later re-classified as the New Army model, and a slightly different version—with changes made in the lock mechanism and in the cylinder locking system—was known later still, from around 1908, as the Colt Army Special. In 1926 the name was changed once again—finally, this time—to Official Police. There was very little difference in type, the change being principally made because at that time the United States police forces were markedly better customers than the United States Army. The arm illustrated is of the orthodox solid-frame design, the frame being of the original ·41in (10·4mm) calibre type. The round barrel has an integral, semi-round foresight and a square backsight notch and groove on the top strap; the upper surface of the latter is matted to reduce the shine. The cylinder swings out sideways on its own yoke when a catch on the left of the frame is pulled back; cartridges or cases can then be ejected simultaneously by pushing the pin. The lock is of rebounding, double-action type, with a separate hammer nose, and access to the mechanism is obtained by way of an irregularly-shaped inspection plate on the left-hand side of the frame. The butt-plates are of chequered walnut.
Very considerable numbers of Official Police revolvers, of which the arm seen here was one, were supplied to the British Army in the course of World War II. It was made also in a ·22in calibre version.

United States of America
## SMITH AND WESSON MILITARY AND POLICE 1ST MOD.

The cut-down revolver seen here had its origins in the Smith and Wesson Military and Police First Model, the company's solid-frame revolver which first appeared in 1899. This example is one of those made for the British Government during World War II, at a time when the hard-pressed British were desperately short of arms and materiel of all kinds. This arm was known variously as the British Service, the Model No 2, or the ·38/200; the latter figure refers to the bullet weight (200 grains, 13 grams) which, by British calculations, provided much the same stopping-power as that fired from the earlier ·455in (11·5mm) calibre Webley service arms (one of which is described on the facing page). In fact, the lead bullet of this type had to be abandoned just before World War II because it contravened the international conventions of warfare; it was replaced by a lighter, 178-grain (11·5 gram), jacketed bullet. As may be seen, the weapon is of orthodox solid-frame type; but it is of interest because at some stage of its career its barrel, which will originally have been 5in (127mm) long, has been cut down to 3·25in (83mm) and a ramp foresight added. The work has been quite well done and it is difficult to detect at a glance. It is, however, clear on closer examination: partly from a certain flatness at the muzzle end, and partly because of the position of the words "SMITH AND WESSON" on the left side of the barrel, which are very close to the new muzzle. The reduction has, of course, had an adverse effect on the revolver's accuracy.

Great Britain
## WEBLEY AND SCOTT Mk VI REVOLVER

P. Webley and Son (later Webley and Scott) had a virtual monopoly on the supply of British Government revolvers for very many years. The company's last, and probably best-known, service arm was the Webley and Scott Mark VI, seen here. It was officially introduced in 1915 and did not differ very much from its predecessors, except that the earlier bird-beak butt had been abandoned in favour of the more conventional squared-off style. It is of standard hinged-frame type, with a robust, stirrup-type, barrel catch: a tough and durable arm, and generally well suited to service use. In the course of World War I, a short bayonet was designed for the revolver; although it was never officially adopted, it proved effective for trench raids and similar operations, and many officers bought one privately. A detachable butt was also provided, but it was not widely used. This model was officially abandoned in 1932 in favour of a similar arm in ·38in (9·6mm) calibre, but many reserve officers still carried Mark VIs in ·455in (11·5mm) calibre when they were recalled in 1939.

*A British police chemist examines a Webley and Scott Mk VI revolver at Preston Forensic Science Lab.*

United States of America
## MERIDEN POCKET REVOLVER

The Meriden Firearms Company was in production from about 1895 until World War I. The weapons produced by the firm were mostly pocket models, including some hammerless versions; and the revolver shown here can probably be classed as a typical specimen. It is of hinged-frame type with a sprung, T-shaped barrel catch (visible in the photograph), the backsight being a simple V-notch in the raised portion of the catch. It has a round barrel with a top rib of slightly peculiar section: it is wider at the top than at its junction with the barrel. Perhaps the only feature of the arm that is in any way remarkable is its somewhat unusual foresight, which has a shape reminiscent of an old-fashioned cocked-hat. The lock is of orthodox double-action type, and the butt-grips are of black vulcanite. It is probably not too unfair to say that this weapon may with justice be classed as cheap and nasty. The workmanship is crude and the components shoddy; but as the price of these revolvers in the early 20th century probably did not exceed a couple of dollars, these low standards are hardly to be wondered at. Such arms, sold extensively by mail order, are often classified as "Suicide Specials" in modern terms. Some arms firms made nothing else, while other, more reputable, companies regarded these weapons as no more than a sideline, and relied on safer and altogether better-quality arms for the bulk of their trade. There is, obviously, still a market for such cheap weapons in the USA, where gun laws are less restrictive.

Brazil
**TAURUS MAGNUM MODEL 86**

| | |
|---|---|
| **Length:** | 9·25" (235mm) |
| **Weight:** | 35oz (·99kg) |
| **Barrel:** | 4" (102mm) |
| **Calibre:** | ·357" Mag (9·06mm) |
| **Rifling:** | 6 groove, r/hand |
| **Capacity:** | Six |
| **Muz Vel:** | c1400 f/s (427 m/s) |
| **Sights:** | Fixed |

Great Britain
**HOME-MADE REVOLVER**

| | |
|---|---|
| **Length:** | 7·5" (190mm) |
| **Weight:** | 25oz (·71kg) |
| **Barrel:** | 3·25" (83mm) |
| **Calibre:** | ·22" (5·6mm) |
| **Rifling:** | Nil |
| **Capacity:** | Six |
| **Muz Vel:** | Not known |
| **Sights:** | Nil |

Brazil
**TAURUS MAGNUM MODEL 86**
This revolver of good quality is chambered for the powerful ·357in (9·06mm) Magnum cartridge (shown here below the barrel), which may be safely fired only in revolvers specially designed for it.

Great Britain
**HOME-MADE REVOLVER**
Few weapons are more dangerous—to the firer—than home-made arms like this. It has no trigger: the spring-loaded hammer must be drawn back manually and then released to fire the ·22in rimfire round.

Great Britain

**WEBLEY Mk IV REVOLVER (DAMAGED)**

| | |
|---|---|
| **Length:** | 11" (279mm) |
| **Weight:** | 36oz (1·02kg) |
| **Barrel:** | 3" (76mm) |
| **Calibre:** | ·455/·476" (11·5/12·1) |
| **Rifling:** | 7 groove, r/hand |
| **Capacity:** | Six |
| **Muz Vel:** | c650 f/s (198 m/s) |
| **Sights:** | Fixed |

Great Britain

**WEBLEY Mk III POLICE AND CIVILIAN**

| | |
|---|---|
| **Length:** | 8·25" (210mm) |
| **Weight:** | 19oz (·54kg) |
| **Barrel:** | 4" (102mm) |
| **Calibre:** | ·38" (9·6mm) |
| **Rifling:** | 7 groove, r/hand |
| **Capacity:** | Six |
| **Muz Vel:** | c600 f/s (183 m/s) |
| **Sights:** | Fixed |

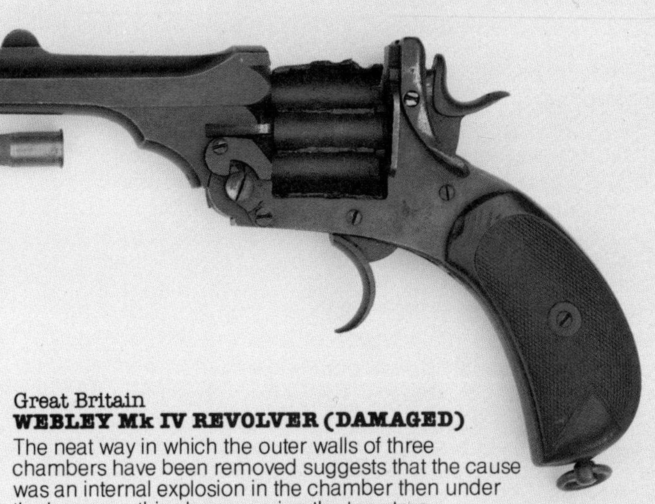

Great Britain

**WEBLEY Mk IV REVOLVER (DAMAGED)**

The neat way in which the outer walls of three chambers have been removed suggests that the cause was an internal explosion in the chamber then under the hammer; this also removing the top strap.

Great Britain

**WEBLEY Mk III POLICE AND CIVILIAN**

This is basically a Government model Webley (like the Mk VI on page 85, top) scaled down from ·455in to ·38in. Its only disadvantage lies in its butt, which is a little too small.

Brazil
## TAURUS MAGNUM MODEL 86

The ·357in (9·06mm) Magnum revolver was originally introduced by Smith and Wesson in 1935, the cartridge being designed in co-operation with Winchester. The Magnum cartridge is about ·1in (2·54mm) longer in the case than the ·38in (9·6mm) Special cartridge, and it may be safely fired only in revolvers specially designed for it. It is popular in the United States, particularly perhaps for game shooting, because of its power and flat trajectory, and it is sometimes used as a rifle cartridge. The weapon illustrated was manufactured by Taurus of Brazil, who began to make revolvers of this calibre in 1975. These arms sell well in the United States and are reputed to be of good quality; certainly, the workmanship and finish of the specimen illustrated leave little to be desired. It is of solid-frame type and has a round barrel with a very wide top rib; the foresight is of ramp type and the arm is fitted with a micrometer backsight, the whole sighting plane being milled to reduce reflection. The cylinder holds six cartridges, the ends of the chambers being recessed to enclose the cartridge heads, and it swings out to the left on its own separate yoke. It has the usual pin-operated extractor; the pin is located in a housing beneath the barrel when the cylinder is in position. There is a separate firing-pin in the standing breech, and the hammer has a wide, flat comb for ease of cocking. The large chequered butt is of two-piece construction and no metal work is visible, except at the back. Small, white-metal medallions in the butt are marked "TAURUS, BRASIL".

Great Britain
## HOME-MADE REVOLVER

This is an example of one of the most dangerous of weapons, a home-made firearm; it can only be described as a monstrosity. The manufacture of cartridges would prove a serious problem for almost anyone, but when factory-made ammunition is obtainable it is not difficult to improvise an instrument with which to fire it. Any person with basic knowledge of metalwork and access to a small workshop can do it—but, this said, it is essential to emphasize that the result is likely to be much more dangerous to the firer than to anyone else. The arm illustrated originated in Northern Ireland, although it is not known whether it was meant for serious use, or whether it is simply the essay of an amateur gunsmith. It has a solid frame of heavy but crude construction. The round barrel has been bored very wide of centre and it is not rifled. The cylinder has a capacity of six and its chambers are counter-sunk to cover the rims of the cartridges. The lump of metal below the cylinder contains a spring plunger; this engages in the circular depressions in the cylinder and thus ensures that the chamber under the hammer is aligned with the barrel. The cylinder itself must be rotated manually. As may be seen, the revolver has no trigger: the hammer is so designed that it must be drawn back by the thumb and then released, when a spring drives it forward with enough force to fire a ·22in (5·6mm) rimfire round. This calibre was presumably chosen because such cartridges are widely used by rifle clubs and are thus relatively easily obtained illegally by the unscrupulous.

Great Britain
## WEBLEY Mk IV REVOLVER (DAMAGED)

The Mark IV Webley service revolver was introduced in 1899 and, as a result, it is frequently referred to as the Boer War model, from its extensive use in that conflict. It was made in a variety of barrel lengths; a 6in (152mm) barrelled version of the Mark V is shown on page 81, top. The arm illustrated here is the Mark IV with a 3in (76mm) barrel. It bears a strong general resemblance to the Mark I, the chief external difference being the lack of swell on the butt behind the hammer. As is immediately apparent from the photograph, this revolver has been the subject of a serious accident: three of its six chambers have been blown out and the top strap has disappeared completely. The trigger-guard is also missing, but this may not be a consequence of the same mishap: since no positive information regarding the circumstances under which this weapon was damaged can be ascertained, it is necessary to speculate. The neat way in which the outer walls of three chambers have been removed suggests that the cause was an internal explosion, possibly in the centre chamber.

*British sailors at revolver drill with the Webley Mk IV, a service arm from 1899 onward.*

Great Britain
## WEBLEY Mk III POLICE AND CIVILIAN

In 1896 Webley introduced a series of ·38in (9·6mm) calibre pocket revolvers, mainly for use by plain-clothes police or civilians. The first model to appear was the Mark II; this came in two sub-types, one with a fixed hammer and the other with a flat-nosed hammer that fell on to a spring-loaded striker on the standing breech. In terms of style, both sub-types followed the general lines of the ·455in (11·5mm) Government models, being simply scaled down for their reduced calibre. The Mark III, introduced almost immediately, differed from the Mark II chiefly in the shape of its butt and in its system of cylinder release. Like the Mark II, it had two types of hammer: the revolver illustrated has a flat-headed hammer with a separate striker. It has an octagonal barrel with a foresight; the backsight is a V-shaped notch on the barrel catch. The latter is of orthodox type, with a thumb lever on the left side of the frame; the V-spring which takes it forward may be clearly seen in the photograph. When the revolver is opened and the barrel forced down, the extractor comes into action in the usual way, throwing out the cartridges or cases. The arm has a double cylinder stop: a forward stop, which works when the hammer is down; and a rear stop, which operates when the trigger is pressed. It is a compact and handy little weapon and proved popular; its only disadvantage lay in its rather smal butt. This fault was rectified in a later model, which first appeared in 1932; this had a very much larger butt and, somewhat unusually, was also fitted with a safety catch.

# Self-Loading Pistols

**Inset:** *British paratroopers—the man at the rear with a 9mm Browning pistol—in action at Oosterbeek, September 1944.*

**Below:** *Men of the US 82nd Airborne Division on the range with Colt Browning Model 1911A1 self-loading pistols.*

When a conventional firearm is discharged the pressure of the expanding gases is evenly distributed, but naturally follows the line of least resistance and forces the projectile up the barrel. The other important direction of pressure is rearward, where, assuming all parts of the arm to be locked rigidly in relation to each other, it manifests itself as recoil or "kick". Ways of harnessing this force were considered early in the history of firearms, but not until the advent of the breechloading arm firing a self-contained metallic cartridge was it possible to translate theory into practice.

In 1883 Maxim produced a successful machine gun. Its barrel was free to recoil for a short distance while remaining locked to the breechblock—this being necessary to allow the internal

*The "gunman" in the centre holds a Mauser Model 1912 pistol —and it is to be hoped that the body-armour being tested by these Washington, DC, policemen in the 1920s was effective!*

pressure to drop to a level where the case would not be ruptured. Once pressure had fallen (which happened quickly) the breech-block unlocked and continued to move rearward, extending a powerful fusee spring which duly provided the motive force to complete the mechanism's forward action.

Maxim's arm was a true automatic: it would continue to fire as long as the trigger was pressed and ammunition was fed in. (Thus, the author prefers to use the term "self-loading pistol", SLP, for what is popularly called an "automatic".) Maxim's first model fired plain lead bullets by means of black powder, but smokeless propellants and jacketed bullets soon appeared. Smokeless propellants gave greatly increased velocity and left comparatively little fouling, but it was found that the extra heat and power tended to distort elongated lead bullets; and by the 1890s bullets had been fitted with thin outer jackets of harder metal to increase their durability. This was most necessary in automatic weapons, where the action of the breech-block was more violent than in manually-operated arms.

### The Borchardt and Mannlicher Systems

The perfection of the small brass centre-fire cartridge, with smokeless powder and a jacketed bullet, made possible the reduction of the self-loading system to a scale applicable to pistols. The first to be reasonably successful commercially, although bulky and difficult to fire with one hand, was made by Hugo Borchardt in 1893. When the first manually-loaded round was fired, the barrel and breechblock recoiled, much as in the Maxim system, until a toggle joint broke upward and allowed them to separate. When the compressed spring thrust the block forward, it stripped the top round from the magazine in the butt and chambered it in preparation for the next shot. The arm's most

**Above:** *Sir Hiram Maxim (1840-1916) whose machine gun of 1883 established the principle of self-loading and automatic arms.*

**Left:** *A German Panzer Grenadier of World War II holds a pistol of unidentified make.*

notable contribution to the development of the SLP was probably its excellent bottle-shaped cartridge, which is still widely used with only minor changes. By 1900, Georg Luger had redeveloped Borchardt's design to the point where he was able to patent it in his own name.

The first of Mannlicher's series of pistols was not in itself a great success; but it led to the establishment of a new functional system in which the rearward thrust of the case forced back an unlocked breechblock. In fact, in the first Mannlicher the barrel moved forward—but in later models the barrel was fixed and the rate of opening of the breechblock was controlled by its weight and by the strength of the return spring. This system gained wide acceptance, and was perfectly reliable for pocket pistols firing relatively low-powered cartridges. In heavier, service-type arms, provision had to be made either to lock the breech briefly or to delay its movement until pressure had fallen to a safe level.

## Bergmann, Mauser and Browning

Theodor Bergmann made effective use of this system in a pocket pistol of 1894 and later produced some military pistols, although these were of recoiling barrel type. The next important SLP was that of Peter Paul Mauser, patented in 1896 and marketed from 1898. It worked on the system of short recoil of the barrel and its locking device, although theoretically less positive than some others, worked very well in practice.

The Mauser had a magazine capacity of ten rounds, compared with a revolver's six, which made it particularly useful for a mounted man. It had a wooden holster which could be attached as a butt: as a carbine it shot fairly well to c.300 yds (270m) and was used in this role by both sides in the Boer War, 1899-1902. Thereafter it sold well worldwide—although in North America the revolver continued to reign supreme.

During World War I Germany modified many Mausers to fire the standard, straight-sided 9mm Parabellum cartridge. When fitted with its detachable butt, the arm proved handy for trench fighting: it may in some measure be regarded as the tactical predecessor of the Bergmann sub-machine gun, which Germany had developed by 1918. A fully automatic Mauser pistol was made between the World Wars, chiefly in Spain: although mechanically reliable, its extremely high rate of fire reduced its accuracy very considerably.

John Browning had produced an effective automatic gun by 1890. Unlike Maxim, who harnessed recoil, Browning tapped off some of the gases produced by the explosion of the charge near the muzzle and used this pressure to activate the working parts. But this action proved somewhat too violent in small, hand-held arms; so Browning reverted to the recoil concept. His first SLP of the new type was made in Belgium in 1899—and in 1900 Colt began to manufacture SLPs based on a Browning patent. This utilized the concept of unlocking the barrel from the breechblock by vertical displacement and, proving highly successful, it was used in almost every pistol made by Colt thereafter and was extensively copied. The fact that a firm of Colt's repute made SLPs ensured their acceptance in the USA—although the revolver retains its great popularity there.

**Below:** *German soldiers on the alert at Arnhem in September 1944 are armed with what appear to be Walther P38 pistols.*

**Below:** *The Colt Model 1911A1 was adopted for US service in 1926. Note the target sight on the example seen here.*

Although excellent SLPs were produced in a number of countries — including various Webley models in Britain; the Roth-Steyr in Austria-Hungary; and the Italian Beretta — Germany never really lost its lead into the 1930s, and German arms were widely copied. The German Walther P38 went a good way towards solving the problem of carrying an SLP safely at instant readiness, by incorporating a double-action lock with an external hammer which could be carried safely in the "down" position with a round in the chamber.

There have been few significant developments since World War II, new models being notable mainly for the use of precision castings and lightweight metals. It may be that, militarily speaking, the pistol is not important enough to warrant much expenditure on its improvement — although a recent upsurge in lawlessness worldwide has redirected attention to the SLP as a weapon for security forces. Although the revolver is more highly favoured, especially in North America, the makers of SLPs may hope to gain ground: a compact, large-calibre arm which can be carried at instant readiness — with the advantage of a magazine capacity of 12-13 rounds — may yet capture a large share of the market.

**Left:** *A British officer of the 9th Lancers in South Africa, 1900, aims a Mauser Model 1896 pistol. This (and the virtually identical Model 1898) were used by both sides in the course of the Boer War of 1899-1902.*

**Below:** *A member of a US Army helicopter transport company in Vietnam, 1964, displays his specially-designed ·22in calibre pistol, complete with muzzle-brake and plastic wood handle.*

Germany
**MAUSER MODEL 1898 SELF-LOADING PISTOL**
With its wooden holster attached to form a stock, as seen here, the Mauser shot reasonably well to around 180-270m (200-300 yds). On the example illustrated, the adjustable leaf backsight is graduated to 450m (492 yds); some went as high as 700m (766 yds).

Germany
**MAUSER MODEL 1898 SELF-LOADING PISTOL**

| | |
|---|---|
| **Length:** | 11·75" (298mm) |
| **Weight:** | 40oz (1·13kg) |
| **Barrel:** | 5·5" (140mm) |
| **Calibre:** | 7·63mm |
| **Rifling:** | 4 groove, r/hand |
| **Capacity:** | Ten |
| **Muz Vel:** | 1400 f/s (427 m/s) |
| **Sights:** | 492 yd (450m) |

Germany
**BORCHARDT SELF-LOADING PISTOL**

| | |
|---|---|
| **Length:** | 13·75" (349mm) |
| **Weight:** | 46oz (1·3kg) |
| **Barrel:** | 6·5" (165mm) |
| **Calibre:** | 7·65mm |
| **Rifling:** | 4 groove, r/hand |
| **Capacity:** | Eight |
| **Muz Vel:** | 1100 f/s (335 m/s) |
| **Sights:** | Fixed |

Germany
**BORCHARDT SELF-LOADING PISTOL**
Like the Mauser (above), the Borchardt was very bulky and was difficult to fire with one hand. It was, therefore, often used with its stock (which incorporates a holster) as a light carbine. Perhaps surprisingly, it does not have an adjustable backsight.

Germany

## MAUSER MODEL 1898 SELF-LOADING PISTOL

The name of Mauser must be among the most famous in the world as far as firearms are concerned. The first bearer of it to achieve fame was Peter Paul Mauser, who was responsible for the famous German Model 1871 rifle which replaced the needle-gun after the Franco-Prussian War. This was followed by a series of progressively better weapons, culminating in the Model 1898 rifle. It is probably no exaggeration to say that, at one time or another, half the armies of the world have been armed with Mauser's products. Mauser first became interested in pistols in the 1870s, and it is probable that his Model 1878 "Zig-Zag" revolver was his first successful hand gun. By the 1890s, the principle of using the recoil of one cartridge to operate the mechanism that loaded the next, established by Hiram Maxim, had become fully accepted. It may, perhaps, have been the appearance of the Borchardt pistol (illustrated below on the colour spread) at about that time that inspired Mauser to try his own hand at a similar arm. What is certain is that his new weapon was based on the 7·65mm Borchardt round (the 7·63mm Mauser cartridge is virtually indentical). The first Mauser self-loading model appeared in 1896 and, with relatively minor improvements, it developed into the Model 1898 pistol seen here. It operates on the short recoil system: the barrel and bolt recoil locked together for a short distance, after which the bolt is unlocked and continues its rearward movement, while the barrel stops. The return spring, which is inside the bolt, is compressed during this rearward travel, which also cocks the hammer. As the force of recoil dies, the compressed spring takes over and drives the bolt forward, picking up a cartridge from the magazine and chambering it on the way. The closure of the bolt locks it to the barrel as it drives it forward —and the pistol is then ready to fire its next round. The hammer, which is cocked in the photograph, strikes an inertia firing-pin in the bolt, which fires the cartridge. Initial cocking is, of course, necessary before the first shot: this is achieved by pulling back the milled ears visible at the rear of the frame. The rounds are fed from a box magazine in front of the trigger-guard, which is initially loaded from a ten-round clip of the type shown. When the last round has been fired, the magazine platform holds the bolt open and thus indicates the need for more ammunition; this system is now the usual one, and the Mauser pistol was the first to feature it. Unlike its predecessor, the Model 1898 is designed to take a stock, which acts also as a holster. It also has an adjustable leaf backsight, which on the weapon seen here is graduated to 450m (492 yds), although the scale on some weapons goes up to 700m (766 yds). Although mechanically reliable, the Mauser never achieved great popularity as a military arm in its early days. Winston Churchill carried one in the Omdurman campaign of 1898, when a shoulder injury prevented him from using a sword effectively, and claimed that it had saved his life, and Mausers were carried by both sides during the South African War of 1899-1902. There, however, long-range rifle fire predominated, and the value of the Mauser was thus limited.

Germany

## BORCHARDT SELF-LOADING PISTOL

Hugo Borchardt was of German birth but went to work in the United States, where he became a naturalized citizen. In the late 1880s he went back to his native country, where he continued to work on a new self-loading pistol. This weapon, which appeared in 1894, may be classed as having been only moderately successful in the commercial sense. It made use of the principle, firstly clearly defined by Maxim, of harnessing the backward thrust of a fired cartridge to reload and recock the weapon. It fired from a locked breech—a system later made famous by Luger—which worked roughly on the principle of the human knee-joint. When it was straight and locked, it was virtually immovable, but as soon as the joint was pushed upward it opened easily and smoothly. When the cartridge was fired, the recoil drove back the barrel and bolt until lugs on the receiver caused the joint to rise, thus allowing it to break. The barrel then stopped, but the bolt continued to the rear against a spring. When the bolt's rearward impetus was exhausted, the compressed spring drove it forward again, stripping a round from the box magazine in the butt and chambering it ready for the next shot. This was the first time such a principle had been applied to a pistol; it worked well, but the weapon was expensive to make, for it called for fine worksmanship and the use of steel of very high quality, especially for the manufacture of the joint pins. The arm was also very bulky, and thus was practically impossible to fire with one hand. To surmount this difficulty, it was provided with a strong and well-fitting stock (which, as may be seen, incorporated a holster): in fact, it seems to have been generally regarded more as a light carbine than as a pistol. Weapons of this type had a certain military value before World War I, since they were suitable for cavalry. The Borchardt fired a powerful cartridge and had a long sight base, which made it reasonably accurate; however, perhaps surprisingly, the backsight was not adjustable. With hindsight, it may be said that what European users really wanted was a weapon constructed on broadly similar principles but small enough to be used as a flat, compact, pocket arm.

*Louis Wessels, leader of a Boer commando in South Africa, 1901, holds a Mauser self-loading pistol with its wooden holster/stock attached.*

Germany
**LUGER ARTILLERY MODEL 1917**
The standard Luger has an eight-round box magazine in the butt, but the example illustrated here is fitted with the so-called "snail-drum" extension magazine, which has a capacity of 32 rounds.

Germany
**MAUSER MODEL 1912**
As reference to pages 98-99 (top) will show, this pistol does not differ significantly from the Model 1898. Many were converted during World War I to fire the 9mm Parabellum cartridge: these are distinguished by a large figure "9" incised into the butt.

Germany
**LUGER ARTILLERY MODEL 1917**

| | |
|---|---|
| **Length:** | 12·75" (324mm) |
| **Weight:** | 37oz (1·05kg) |
| **Barrel:** | 7·5" (190mm) |
| **Calibre:** | 9mm |
| **Rifling:** | 6 groove, r/hand |
| **Capacity:** | 8 (box)/32 (drum) |
| **Muz Vel:** | 1250 f/s (380 m/s) |
| **Sights:** | 875 yd (800m) |

Germany
**MAUSER MODEL 1912**

| | |
|---|---|
| **Length:** | 11·75" (298mm) |
| **Weight:** | 44oz (1·25kg) |
| **Barrel:** | 5·5" (140mm) |
| **Calibre:** | 7·63mm |
| **Rifling:** | 6 groove, r/hand |
| **Capacity:** | Ten |
| **Muz Vel:** | 1400 f/s (427 m/s) |
| **Sights:** | 1094 yd (1000m) |

A Mauser Model 1912 converted to fire the 9mm Parabellum cartridge: note the deeply-incised figure "9" in the butt.

Germany
## LUGER ARTILLERY MODEL 1917

The Luger Parabellum self-loading pistol had its origins in the Borchardt, which was developed by Georg Luger. It proved successful and was adopted by the German Army in 1908; this naturally ensured that it would be generally accepted, and its subsequent record in World War I made it a household name: the name of Luger is equally as famous as that of Mauser. A long-barrelled commercial model was produced in 1903-1904, and this was soon adopted as the standard pistol of the German Navy. In 1917, this was followed in its turn by the Artillery Model, illustrated here. Like its parent arm, the Borchardt, the Luger works on a system of short recoil, during which the barrel and bolt remain locked together. The toggle joint then passes over curved ramps and opens upward, detaching itself from the barrel. When the bolt has reached its rearmost position, it is forced forward again by a return spring, stripping a cartridge from the magazine and forcing it into the chamber en route. It then locks, and may be fired again in the normal way. The standard Luger has a box magazine in the butt, but the example seen here is fitted with an extension type, the so-called "snail drum" magazine with a capacity of 32 rounds. A special tool was needed to load this magazine, which tended to jam; this was cured by replacing the original round-nosed bullet with a pointed one. As may be seen, the Luger also had a detachable stock, which converted it into a carbine and made it a very light and handy weapon for local defence. It was originally issued to machine gun detachments and artillery observers in exposed forward positions. As stocks of the arm increased, it was also issued to non-commissioned officers of forward infantry units, where, like the Mauser, it was found to be a very handy arm for such work as night raids. Although Germany cannot really be said to have invented the sub-machine gun, it was probably the success of the German self-loading pistols which encouraged the country to develop the automatic Bergmann.

*A steel-helmeted Bulgarian officer, in 1918, holds a Luger P08; the Artillery Model was a long-barrelled (7·5in; 190mm) variant.*

Germany
## MAUSER MODEL 1912

Some details of the origins and history of the early Mauser pistols have already been given on pages 100-101. The Model 1898 was followed by others in 1903 and 1905; but at one time it seemed possible that these might be the last of the series. Mauser had begun making experiments in other fields, notably with a new breech locking system which was used both in a self-loading pistol and in a rifle. Only a few Model 06/08 pistols embodying this system were produced; all were chambered for the 9mm Mauser "Export" cartridge. However, Mauser soon returned to work on his earlier series, and yet another self-loading pistol, the Model 1912, illustrated here, duly appeared. It did not differ significantly from its predecessor of 14 years before. Weapons of this type were, of course, made by the thousand for use in World War I and, not surprisingly, they are still numerous. In 1916 the German Army had a requirement for Mauser pistols to fire the straight-sided 9mm Parabellum cartridge, and it was quickly realized that conversion of the standard Model 1912 would be relatively simple. The arms thus altered were all distinguished by a large figure "9", cut into the butt-grips and painted red. The Mauser pistol was widely used in World War I because, unlike many earlier 20th-century campaigns, it involved a good deal of close-quarter fighting. The emphasis as far as the infantry was concerned was, of course, on the rifle, light machine gun and medium machine gun; nevertheless, it was found that a Mauser pistol with its shoulder-stock attached was a handy weapon for raids, clearing trenches, and similar operations. It was used in very similar fashion to the sub-machine gun which the Germans finally adopted in 1918. A Mauser-type pistol with a capability for automatic fire was, in fact, made in Spain in the 1930s. However, the combination of a light bolt travelling over a very short distance and a powerful cartridge was not successful, and the arm's rate of fire made it impossible to shoot with very much accuracy.

*The 7·63mm Mauser Model 1912, here held by an American police officer, is outwardly almost identical with the Model 1898.*

Germany
**BERGMANN-BAYARD SELF-LOADING PISTOL**

| | |
|---|---|
| **Length:** | 9·9" (251mm) |
| **Weight:** | 35·5oz (1·01kg) |
| **Barrel:** | 4" (102mm) |
| **Calibre:** | 9mm |
| **Rifling:** | 6 groove, l/hand |
| **Capacity:** | Six |
| **Muz Vel:** | c1000 f/s (305 m/s) |
| **Sights:** | Fixed |

Germany
**SCHWARZLOSE MODEL 1908**

| | |
|---|---|
| **Length:** | 9·2" (234mm) |
| **Weight:** | 32oz (·91kg) |
| **Barrel:** | 4·75" (121mm) |
| **Calibre:** | 9mm |
| **Rifling:** | 4 groove, r/hand |
| **Capacity:** | Six |
| **Muz Vel:** | c1000 f/s (305 m/s) |
| **Sights:** | Fixed |

Germany
**BERGMANN-BAYARD SELF-LOADING PISTOL**
This was the first European pistol of its kind to fire the powerful 9mm cartridge. To improve long range accuracy, military models were often fitted with a detachable holster-stock of hard leather.

Germany
**SCHWARZLOSE MODEL 1908**
Note the metal arm in front of the butt. This is a grip safety: unless it is firmly gripped by a hand in the proper firing position, the trigger will not function. A stud on the left side of the butt, however, allows the safety to be locked in if desired.

Belgium
**BROWNING MODEL 1900 ("OLD MODEL")**

| | |
|---|---|
| **Length:** | 6·4" (163mm) |
| **Weight:** | 22oz (·62kg) |
| **Barrel:** | 4" (102mm) |
| **Calibre:** | 7·65mm |
| **Rifling:** | 5 groove, r/hand |
| **Capacity:** | Seven |
| **Muz Vel:** | c850 f/s (259 m/s) |
| **Sights:** | Fixed |

Denmark
**DANSK SCHOUBOE MODEL 1907**

| | |
|---|---|
| **Length:** | 8·8" (224mm) |
| **Weight:** | 42oz (1·19kg) |
| **Barrel:** | 5" (127mm) |
| **Calibre:** | 11·35mm |
| **Rifling:** | 6 groove, r/hand |
| **Capacity:** | Six |
| **Muz Vel:** | c1600 f/s (488 m/s) |
| **Sights:** | Fixed |

Belgium
**BROWNING MODEL 1900 ("OLD MODEL")**
This was the first self-loading pistol produced by the great John Browning—a robust and reliable weapon. Although it was made only between 1900 and 1912 (in Belgium, like almost all Browning's self-loaders), many examples are still to be found.

Denmark
**DANSK SCHOUBOE MODEL 1907**
Schouboe designed a light-weight bullet to minimise the weight of his pistol—but this led to a serious lack of stopping-power.

Germany
## BERGMANN-BAYARD SELF-LOADING PISTOL

Although the German gunmaker Theodor Bergmann was responsible for a number of ingenious developments, it is possible that he was himself more of a businessman than an innovator and relied on other people for technical assistance. In 1901 he produced the Bergmann-Bayard pistol seen here. It was designed specifically as a military arm, originally under the trade-name "Mars", and was the first European pistol of its kind to fire a 9mm cartridge, which was a very powerful round. The Spanish Army put in a considerable order, but Bergmann had trouble with contractors and few, if any, pistols were ever actually supplied by him. He eventually sold the rights to Pieper of Liège, who completed the order and also sold some of these arms to the Greek and Danish Armies. Once these orders were completed, Pieper put an improved version on the market. The pistol works on a system of short recoil. Barrel and bolt recoil together for about 0·25in (6mm); the barrel stops; and the bolt is unlocked by being forced downward and continues to the rear, extracting the empty case (if any) and compressing the return spring which is contained within it, coiled round the long striker. On its forward movement, the bolt strips a cartridge from the magazine in front of the trigger-guard and chambers it in readiness for the next shot. The pistol was considered to be clumsy in use, and recoil from its powerful cartridge was considerable. Military models were often fitted with a detachable holster stock of hard leather.

Germany
## SCHWARZLOSE MODEL 1908

Andreas Schwarzlose is perhaps best remembered as the inventor of a medium machine gun with a simple but effective blowback action instead of a more complex locked breech. Its reliability was confirmed by its adoption by Austria in World War I and by Italy in World War II. Schwarzlose's real interest, however, was in self-loading pistols, and from 1892 onward he produced a variety of ingenious mechanisms. Perhaps unfortunately for Schwarzlose, the Mauser was fairly well established by the time that his arms appeared, and thus they never really had the success they deserved. However, he persevered, and by 1908 he had produced this pistol. It is, in many ways, a remarkable arm: perhaps its most interesting feature is that the usual blowback system has been replaced by a blow-forward mechanism. The breech-block is an integral part of the frame, but the barrel is mounted on ribs and is therefore free to be forced forward by the explosion of the charge; this leaves the empty case held in an ejector, which throws it clear mechanically. On its forward movement, the barrel stretches a heavy recoil spring; when its forward impetus is exhausted, the spring draws it backward, scooping the next round from the magazine and also cocking the hammer. The metal arm in front of the butt is a grip safety: it must be firmly gripped, in the proper firing position, or the trigger will not function. There is, however, a stud on the left side of the butt which allows the safety to be locked in, if necessary.

Belgium
## BROWNING MODEL 1900 ("OLD MODEL")

John Moses Browning is one of the greatest names in the entire history of firearms, and his work on self-loading weapons of all types, ranging from medium machine guns to small pocket pistols, is unsurpassed. His first successful venture was a machine gun made by the Colt company and adopted by the United States Navy in 1898; it was not until two years later that he finally produced a self-loading pistol, of the type shown here. However, after a disagreement with the American gunmaker Winchester, with whom he had worked for some years, Browning came to the conclusion that more interest might be shown in his self-loading pistol in Europe than in the United States—where the revolver was almost universally predominant. In this he was right: the great Belgian firm of Fabrique Nationale ("FN"), Liège, showed immediate interest, and the weapon was soon in production in great quantity. It is robust, reliable and mechanically simple; and although it has not been made since 1912, many are still to be found. The barrel is fastened to the frame; above it is a moving slide which contains the recoil spring. The slide must, of course, be operated manually to load the first round. When this is fired, gas pressure forces the empty case backward, taking with it the breechblock and slide and compressing the recoil spring, which also operates the striker. The spring then takes over and forces the whole assembly forward, stripping a cartridge from the box magazine in the butt and chambering it in preparation for the next shot.

Denmark
## DANSK SCHOUBOE MODEL 1907

Lieutenant Jens Torring Schouboe was an officer in the Danish Army and also, apparently, a director of the Dansk Rekylriffel Syndikat; he was closely involved with the development of the famous Madsen light machine gun. In 1903, Schouboe patented a self-loading pistol, but although it was well made and reliable, it failed to sell. He therefore decided that what was needed was a heavier arm of the same general type but of service calibre, and this he set out to achieve, the result being the weapon illustrated here. Like his earlier arms, this was of simple blowback design, without any breech-locking mechanism—but while this type of action is easy enough to incorporate into small pocket pistols firing low-powered cartridges, it is very hard to do so in a service-type arm without making it extremely heavy. Schouboe's answer to this problem was to produce a cartridge firing an extremely lightweight bullet which, he reasoned, would not only reduce recoil but would also leave the barrel faster, thus reducing the period of maximum pressure. The bullet was basically a wooden round with a thin metal jacket. Schouboe's solution worked: the weapon was very satisfactory from the purely mechanical point of view—but it had two serious defects as a military arm. The first was that the bullet was too light to have very much stopping-power; the second was that it lost accuracy very quickly, presumably for the same reason. Although Schouboe produced improved versions, it was never popular and ceased manufacture in 1917.

Great Britain
**WEBLEY No 1 Mk I**

| | |
|---|---|
| **Length:** | 8·5" (216mm) |
| **Weight:** | 39oz (1·1kg) |
| **Barrel:** | 5" (127mm) |
| **Calibre:** | ·455" |
| **Rifling:** | 7 groove, r/hand |
| **Capacity:** | Seven |
| **Muz Vel:** | c750 f/s (229 m/s) |
| **Sights:** | Fixed |

Great Britain
**WEBLEY AND SCOTT MODEL 1904**

| | |
|---|---|
| **Length:** | 10" (254mm) |
| **Weight:** | 48oz (1·36kg) |
| **Barrel:** | 6·5" (165mm) |
| **Calibre:** | ·455" |
| **Rifling:** | 7 groove, r/hand |
| **Capacity:** | Seven |
| **Muz Vel:** | c750 f/s (229 m/s) |
| **Sights:** | Fixed |

Great Britain
**WEBLEY No 1 Mk I**
This arm was officially adopted as the standard pistol of the Royal Navy in 1913. A Mark II, with a stock, was issued to the Royal Flying Corps until the introduction of the aerial machine gun.

Great Britain
**WEBLEY AND SCOTT MODEL 1904**
The noticeably square configuration of the first in the series, which went on the market in 1904, was to become a characteristic of all self-loading pistols made by the firm of Webley and Scott.

Great Britain
**WEBLEY MODEL 1909**

| | |
|---|---|
| **Length:** | 8" (203mm) |
| **Weight:** | 34oz (·96kg) |
| **Barrel:** | 5" (127mm) |
| **Calibre:** | ·38" |
| **Rifling:** | 7 groove, r/hand |
| **Capacity:** | Seven |
| **Muz Vel:** | c750 f/s (229 m/s) |
| **Sights:** | Fixed |

Great Britain
**WEBLEY-MARS**

| | |
|---|---|
| **Length:** | 12·25" (311mm) |
| **Weight:** | 48oz (1·36kg) |
| **Barrel:** | 9·5" (241mm) |
| **Calibre:** | ·38" |
| **Rifling:** | 7 groove, r/hand |
| **Capacity:** | Seven |
| **Muz Vel:** | 1750 f/s (533 m/s) |
| **Sights:** | Fixed |

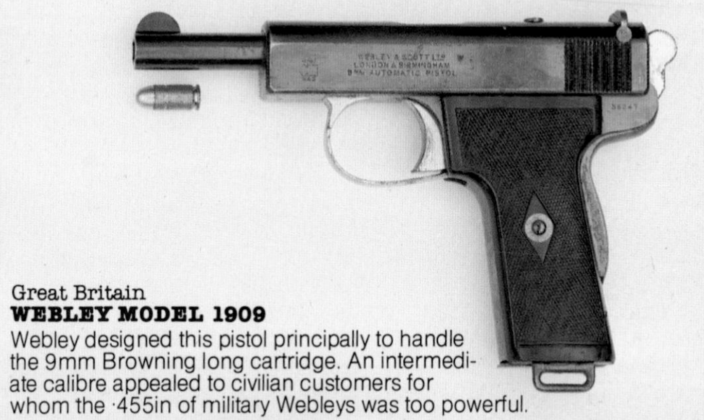

Great Britain
**WEBLEY MODEL 1909**
Webley designed this pistol principally to handle the 9mm Browning long cartridge. An intermediate calibre appealed to civilian customers for whom the ·455in of military Webleys was too powerful.

Great Britain
**WEBLEY-MARS**
This enormous and well-constructed arm, which was made in both ·45in and ·38in calibre, is now probably the rarest of all self-loading pistols. Mechanically complex, it was tested by the British Army in 1901-03 but failed to gain acceptance.

Great Britain
## WEBLEY No 1 Mk I

After the Webley and Scott Model 1904, the firm's next full-bored model was the No 1 Mk I, developed from c1906, which became the standard pistol of the Royal Navy in 1913. A heavy and robust arm with all the Webley characteristics, it works by recoil. When a loaded magazine is inserted into the butt and the slide is pulled back and released, a round is chambered and the hammer is cocked. At the moment of firing, the barrel is locked to the slide—a lug on the barrel engaging in a recess in the upper part of the slide—and the two recoil briefly together. Once the gas pressure has dropped to a safe level (a process that is measured in thousandths of a second) the barrel is forced downward by a cam-way and disengages from the slide, which continues to the rear, cocking the hammer as it does so. The slide's forward movement, under the impetus of the V-spring behind the right butt-plate, strips the top round from the magazine and chambers it. A Mark II version, fitted with a stock, was issued to the Royal Flying Corps.

*Royal Naval Air pilots, World War I: those nearest the camera have Webley No 1 Mk I SLPs.*

Great Britain
## WEBLEY AND SCOTT MODEL 1904

By the end of the 19th century it had become clear that the self-loading pistol had a future. Much of the work of development was done in Western Europe and, initially, neither the United States nor Great Britain showed much interest. But the new system could not be ignored completely, and as early as 1898 Webley and Scott had sought a suitable design. Apart from the Webley-Mars, which is illustrated on page 111, bottom, the firm found nothing to its liking until the model illustrated here, which first went on to the market in 1904. As may be seen, it is of the characteristically square style which was later to become a noticeable feature of all Webley and Scott pistols of this type. It fires a powerful cartridge which necessitates a locked breech. The barrel and breech block remain locked on initial recoil until a vertical bolt drops and allows them to separate. The V-shaped recoil spring is situated under the right butt-plate. Overall, the weapon is of rather complex design; it is, perhaps, *too* well made, and is said to have been susceptible to stoppages caused by dirt. However, it set the style for Webley self-loaders.

Great Britain
## WEBLEY MODEL 1909

In 1908, Webley began work on a pistol of international calibre, to meet the needs of civilian customers who did not require anything quite as powerful as the full-sized ·455in cartridge used in the firm's various military models. The new weapon was on the market by 1909. It was designed principally to handle the 9mm Browning long cartridge, which had been introduced initially for the 1903 Browning pistol made by Fabrique Nationale. This round was of fair velocity and provided adequate stopping-power: it was popular in many parts of the world for civilian and police use, although it was not widely employed in the United States. The round was not sufficiently powerful to necessitate a locked breech, so it was possible for the arm to be of a simple blowback design. The first round must be manually loaded in the usual way, but when it is fired it blows back the slide, cocks the hammer and compresses the recoil spring in the butt. The spring then drives the action forward and strips and chambers the next cartridge. In this model, the barrel is held in position by a lug on top of the trigger-guard, which is pulled forward to strip the weapon. The earliest versions had a safety catch on the left-hand side of the frame, but later examples have a grip safety at the back of the butt, as seen in the photograph. When the safety is out, the sear cannot engage, but when the butt is firmly gripped, the sear is forced into position so that the weapon can be fired. The Model 1909 was adopted by the South African Police in 1920 and production did not end until 1930.

Great Britain
## WEBLEY-MARS

The originator of this pistol was Hugh Gabbet-Fairfax, who took out a variety of patents on self-loading pistols in the period 1895-1900. In 1898 he submitted a design to the famous Birmingham firm of Webley and Scott, which was then seeking a suitable design for a self-loading arm. The firm did not wish to adopt this particular model under its own name, but agreed to manufacture it for the inventor, presumably on a commission basis. The British Army tested it in the period 1901-03 but finally did not adopt it. This adverse decision appears to have been due partly to the arm's heavy recoil, and partly to its persistent tendency either to fail to eject empty cases—or to eject them into the firer's face. Although, in 1902, Gabbet-Fairfax decided that the latter fault was due to defective ammunition, and promised a new batch in which this would be rectified, the whole project had to be abandoned. Gabbet-Fairfax, who had borrowed a great deal of money to develop the Mars, then went bankrupt; a new company was formed, briefly and unsuccessfully, in the period 1904-07. The Webley-Mars is a huge arm and was designed to fire a powerful bottle-necked cartridge. Although it is extremely well made, it is mechanically complex, since the cartridge necessitates a robust system of locking the bolt to the barrel at the moment of firing. This is done by arranging for the bolt to turn so that four lugs on it engage in recesses behind the chamber. When a shot is fired, the barrel and bolt at first recoil together, until the latter turns and unlocks itself.

Germany
**BERGMANN 1896 (No 3)**

| | |
|---|---|
| **Length:** | 10" (254mm) |
| **Weight:** | 40oz (1·13kg) |
| **Barrel:** | 4" (102mm) |
| **Calibre:** | 7·63mm |
| **Rifling:** | 4 groove, r/hand |
| **Capacity:** | Five |
| **Muz Vel:** | c1250 f/s (380 m/s) |
| **Sights:** | Fixed |

Germany
**BERGMANN 1897 (No 5)**

| | |
|---|---|
| **Length:** | 10·5" (267mm) |
| **Weight:** | 26·5oz (·75kg) |
| **Barrel:** | 4·4" (112mm) |
| **Calibre:** | 7·63mm |
| **Rifling:** | 4 groove, r/hand |
| **Capacity:** | Five |
| **Muz Vel:** | c1100 f/s (335 m/s) |
| **Sights:** | 765 yd (700m) |

Germany
**BERGMANN 1896 (No 3)**
The cartridges used in earlier Bergmann pistols were rimless and sharply tapered to avoid sticking. Later models, with mechanical extractors, used cartridges with grooved rims, as illustrated here.

Germany
**BERGMANN 1897 (No 5)**
Britain, among other countries, experimented with but rejected the Bergmann No 5. Its bullet weight was considered to be too light—with consequent loss of accuracy and stopping-power—for service use.

Austria-Hungary
**MANNLICHER MODEL 1901**

| | |
|---|---|
| **Length:** | 9·4" (239mm) |
| **Weight:** | 33oz (·94kg) |
| **Barrel:** | 6·5" (165mm) |
| **Calibre:** | 7·63mm |
| **Rifling:** | 4 groove, r/hand |
| **Capacity:** | Eight |
| **Muz Vel:** | 1025 f/s (312 m/s) |
| **Sights:** | Fixed |

Austria-Hungary
**MANNLICHER MODEL 1903**

| | |
|---|---|
| **Length:** | 10·5" (267mm) |
| **Weight:** | 35oz (·99kg) |
| **Barrel:** | 4·5" (114mm) |
| **Calibre:** | 7·65mm |
| **Rifling:** | 5 groove, r/hand |
| **Capacity:** | Six |
| **Muz Vel:** | c1090 f/s (332 m/s) |
| **Sights:** | Fixed |

Austria-Hungary
**MANNLICHER MODEL 1901**
When the small milled catch above the right butt-plate is pressed, the spring of the magazine—which is integral with the arm and is loaded by charger from the top—forces out unexpended rounds.

Austria-Hungary
**MANNLICHER MODEL 1903**
The curved lever seen here above the trigger of the final Mannlicher model is an external cocking device. The arm is cocked for the first shot by drawing back the milled knob on top of the frame.

Germany
## BERGMANN 1896 (No 3)

Theodor Bergmann's first patent for a self-loading pistol dates back to 1892. By 1894 he had developed a reasonably successful arm, of which an improved version, appearing in 1896, was the weapon illustrated. It is a well-made arm of simple blowback type; perhaps its main point of interest (in the early versions) is its complete lack of any mechanical system of extraction or ejection. In fact the action is so designed that the bolt opens while there is still sufficient gas available to blow the cartridge case out backwards. The case then strikes the next round in the magazine, and, in theory at least, bounces clear—although in practice this process is somewhat unpredictable. A gas escape port in the chamber serves as a safety device should the case rupture under pressure. The early cartridges had no rim of any kind and were quite sharply tapered to avoid any risk of sticking. However, the system was not considered to be reliable, and later versions were fitted with mechanical extractors, necessitating the use of cartridges with grooved rims. The pistol is loaded by pulling down and forward on the milled grip by the trigger-guard, which opens the magazine cover. A five-round clip is inserted and the cover is closed. A lifter spring pushes the rounds up under the bolt one by one and the empty clip is finally ejected downwards. Rounds can be loaded without the clip, but the feed system is by no means reliable in this case, since the rounds are liable to become displaced. The pistol is sometimes referred to as the Bergmann "No 3".

Germany
## BERGMANN 1897 (No 5)

Although the 1896 model in the Bergmann series worked fairly well, it did not achieve real popularity; principally, perhaps, because it was somewhat less effective than the Mauser which came on to the market at about the same time. Apart from small, pocket arms, it was by then clear that the main requirement for self-loading pistols would be for military versions—and as these were always required to fire a powerful cartridge, it was necessary that they should fire with the breech locked. If this was not done, the cartridge case would be pushed out of the chamber when gas pressure was still high and, unsupported by the walls of the chamber, it was likely to rupture. In 1897, therefore, Bergmann patented a pistol of the type seen here. In this design the barrel and bolt are locked together at the instant of firing and remain so during the first ·24in (6mm) of recoil. A cam in the frame then forces the bolt slightly sideways and unlocks it from the barrel, which then stops. The bolt continues to the rear, to cock the hammer, and then comes forward, strips a round from the magazine, chambers it, locks on to the barrel, and forces it back to its forward firing position. The magazine is of detachable box type, incorporating its own platform and spring. The pistol may, however, also be loaded through the top of the frame by means of a charger. Much to Bergmann's disappointment, no country adopted this arm, although several experimented with it. Britain rejected it because its bullet weight was considered to be too light.

Austria-Hungary
## MANNLICHER MODEL 1901

Joseph Werndl founded an arms factory at Steyr, Austria, in 1834. His son (also Joseph) went to the USA in search of contracts during the Civil War; he was so impressed with American production methods that on his return he completely modernized his Steyr factory—and was soon making military small arms for the Austrian government and others. Steyr's first self-loading pistols were made in 1894 to the design of Ferdinand, Ritter von Mannlicher, a German-born designer perhaps now best remembered for his excellent military rifles. Several models were made over the next few years; the arm illustrated here is the Model 1901. As is to be expected from a factory with the high reputation of Steyr, the weapon is very well made and finished. It is basically of blowback design but of the type usually known as retarded blowback. There is no positive locked-breech system: the rearward movement of the slide is mechanically retarded for a very brief period to ensure that the gas pressure in the barrel falls to a safe level. This system also incidentally permitted the use of a relatively light slide without engendering excessive recoil. Although the magazine is located in the butt—in the style familiar on modern arms—it is not, in fact, a detachable box but an integral part of the arm; and it is loaded from the top by means of a charger. If the user desires to empty the magazine, the slide is drawn back and pressure is put on the small milled catch (visible in the photograph) above the right butt-plate; this allows the magazine spring to force out the unexpended rounds.

Austria-Hungary
## MANNLICHER MODEL 1903

This pistol appeared on the market in 1903, and was the last type of Mannlicher to be produced. Like most other firms concerned with self-loading arms, Mannlicher obviously realized that the future of such weapons lay in the military sphere; thus, development should be concerned with weapons firing powerful cartridges from locked-breech systems. The Mannlicher Model 1903, seen here, is of that type. It is cocked for the first shot by drawing back the bolt by means of the milled knob visible on top of the frame. When released, the bolt goes forward, stripping a cartridge from the magazine and chambering it. When the bolt is fully forward, a bolt-stop rises from the frame and supports it while the round is fired. Then barrel and bolt recoil for about ·2in (5mm), after which the bolt-stop falls. The barrel now stops, but the bolt continues backward to complete the recocking and reloading cycle in readiness for the next shot. The pistol has an internal hammer which acts on the firing pin; it also has an external cocking device in the form of the curved lever visible above the trigger. The magazine is of box type and can be removed by pressing in a small catch on the front of the trigger-guard, which allows it to drop down. The small milled catch at the back of the frame is the safety. Perhaps the most remarkable aspect of this weapon is that although it fires a cartridge of the same dimensions as the Mauser, the actual charge is less: thus, the Mannlicher is not considered safe to fire the 7·65mm Mauser round.

Germany/Belgium
**BERGMANN SIMPLEX**

| | |
|---|---|
| **Length:** | 7·5" (190mm) |
| **Weight:** | 21oz (·59kg) |
| **Barrel:** | 2·75" (70mm) |
| **Calibre:** | 8mm |
| **Rifling:** | 6 groove, r/hand |
| **Capacity:** | Six or Eight |
| **Muz Vel:** | c650 f/s (198 m/s) |
| **Sights:** | Fixed |

Austria-Hungary
**ROTH-STEYR MODEL 1907**

| | |
|---|---|
| **Length:** | 9" (229mm) |
| **Weight:** | 36oz (1·02kg) |
| **Barrel:** | 5" (127mm) |
| **Calibre:** | 8mm |
| **Rifling:** | 4 groove, r/hand |
| **Capacity:** | Ten |
| **Muz Vel:** | 1090 f/s (332 m/s) |
| **Sights:** | Fixed |

Germany/Belgium
**BERGMANN SIMPLEX**
Although of characteristic Bergmann shape, the Simplex is notably smaller than the designer's other weapons: it was originated as a pocket pistol, firing a specially-designed 8mm cartridge.

Austria-Hungary
**ROTH-STEYR MODEL 1907**
This was the first self-loading pistol to replace a revolver as an official service arm with a major power. It was adopted by the Austro-Hungarian Army, largely for use as a cavalry weapon, in 1907.

Hungary
**FROMMER MODEL 1910**

| | |
|---|---|
| **Length:** | 7·25" (184mm) |
| **Weight:** | 21oz (·59kg) |
| **Barrel:** | 4·25" (108mm) |
| **Calibre:** | 7·65mm |
| **Rifling:** | 5 groove, r/hand |
| **Capacity:** | Seven |
| **Muz Vel:** | c1100 f/s (335 m/s) |
| **Sights:** | Fixed |

Austria-Hungary
**STEYR MODEL 1911**

| | |
|---|---|
| **Length:** | 8·5" (216mm) |
| **Weight:** | 35oz (·99kg) |
| **Barrel:** | 5·1" (130mm) |
| **Calibre:** | ·357" |
| **Rifling:** | 4 groove, r/hand |
| **Capacity:** | Eight |
| **Muz Vel:** | c1100 f/s (335 m/s) |
| **Sights:** | Fixed |

Hungary
**FROMMER MODEL 1910**
Unlike earlier Frommer pistols, which had integral magazines, the Model 1910 is fitted with a detachable seven-round box magazine. Note the grip safety at the rear of the pistol's butt.

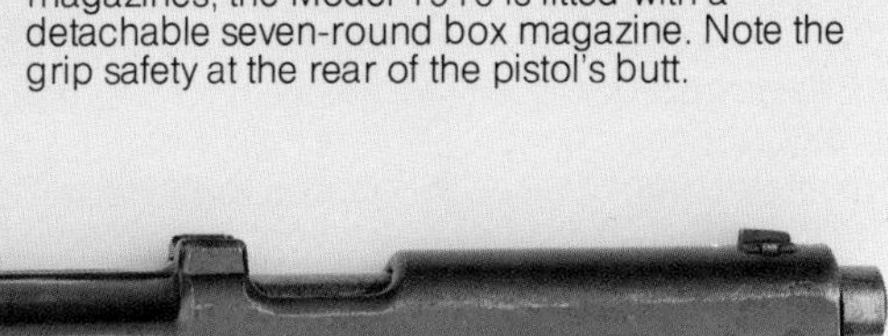

Austria-Hungary
**STEYR MODEL 1911**
This solid, square-seeming arm bears some external resemblance to the famous Colt Model 1911 (see page 123, top), its exact contemporary. It was the official Austro-Hungarian pistol in World War I.

Germany/Belgium

## BERGMANN SIMPLEX

The Bergmann Simplex pistol was patented in 1901. A few were made in Austria, but in 1904 the design was licensed to a company in Belgium, which thereafter turned the arm out in quite large numbers until 1914, when production finally ceased. Although the general shape of the weapon characterizes it as being obviously of Bergmann origin, its scale is much smaller than that of the designer's other weapons: the Simplex was originated strictly as a pocket arm. It fired a specially-designed cartridge (which is no longer available) and, because it was of low power, it was possible to design the weapon on the blowback principle, with no need for a locked breech. The pistol is cocked by pulling back the bolt by means of the cylindrical cocking-piece, visible just in front of the hammer. When released, the bolt goes forward under its recoil spring, strips a round from the magazine and chambers it ready to fire; after the first shot the process is repeated automatically. The lock is a simple single-action revolver type. The weapon has a detachable box magazine in front of the trigger in the orthodox arrangement: it is removed by pressing the small stud on the front of the magazine housing, which allows it to drop downward. On Belgian-made examples, the barrel is screwed into the frame; whereas the original Austrian arms had their barrels forged integrally. The Bergmann is simple and reliable: it sold well as a pocket pistol, although the fact that it required a special cartridge must have been to some extent a limiting factor on its use.

Austria-Hungary

## ROTH-STEYR MODEL 1907

This pistol first went into full production in 1907, when it was taken into service by the Austro-Hungarian Army, mainly for use as a cavalry arm. This was the first occasion on which any major power adopted a self-loading pistol in place of a revolver. The Roth-Steyr pistol fires from a locked breech —and this mechanism is of a very unusual type. The bolt is very long: its rear end is solid, except for a sleeve for the striker, but its front part is hollow and is of sufficient diameter to fit closely over the barrel. The interior of the bolt has cam grooves cut into it, and the barrel has studs of appropriate size to fit the grooves. When the pistol is fired, the barrel and bolt recoil together within the hollow receiver for about ·5in (12·7mm). During this operation, the grooves in the bolt cause the barrel to turn through 90 degrees, after which it is held while the bolt continues to the rear, cocking the action as it does so. On its forward journey, the bolt picks up a cartridge through a slot on its lower surface and chambers it, while the action of the studs in the grooves turns the barrel back to its locked position. The magazine, which is in the butt, is an integral part of the weapon and is loaded from a clip. Although this pistol was given the name of Georg Roth, he was, in fact, responsible for the design of the ammunition (for this and for Steyr arms in other calibres) rather than of the weapon itself. Credit for the design of the pistol is assigned to Karel Krnka, who worked with Roth from 1898 until shortly before the latter's death in 1909.

Hungary
## FROMMER MODEL 1910

Rudolf Frommer worked for many years at the Royal Hungarian Arsenal, Fegyvergyar. His first pistol, of 1903, was generally considered to be far too complex for military use. However, he continued to simplify the design, and by 1910 had produced the pistol illustrated here. It is of a most unusual type: it works on the principle of long recoil, in which the barrel and bolt remain locked together for the whole of the rearward phase of movement. Under this system, the barrel only becomes unlocked from the rotating head of the bolt as the barrel resumes its forward movement, the bolt being held briefly to the rear by a stop. Extraction and ejection take place during this forward movement: as the barrel reaches the proper position, it trips the bolt stop and allows the bolt to go forward, stripping a round from the magazine, chambering it, and simultaneously locking back on to the barrel by the rotation of its head. This movement of the barrel and bolt necessitated the incorporation of two separate recoil springs to drive them back into position. The earlier Frommer pistols had integral magazines which were loaded through the top of the frame by means of a clip, but this Model 1910 has a separate, detachable, box magazine. The weapon has a large inspection plate on the left-hand side of the frame: access to the mechanism is obtained by turning and pushing in the circular stud just in front of the hammer, which forces the plate outward. The pistol has a grip safety (seen at the back of the butt).

Austria-Hungary
## STEYR MODEL 1911

As far as hand guns were concerned, Steyr's chief endeavour in the early years of the 20th century appears to have been to produce an acceptable self-loading pistol of military type. This the firm accomplished with the appearance of the Model 1911 pistol illustrated here. It is a solid, square looking arm with some external resemblance to the famous Colt self-loader (see page 123, top) of the same year. It has the same heavy slide, with the barrel inside it, which covers the whole of the frame. When the action is in the forward position, two lugs on the top of the barrel engage in two corresponding slots in the slide. When the slide is drawn back for initial loading, the barrel moves with it for a short distance and is rotated sufficiently to disengage it from the slots. The barrel then stops, but the slide continues to the rear and cocks the hammer. It then moves forward, driven by the recoil spring, stripping a round from the magazine and chambering it. During this forward movement, the barrel rotates back into the locked position in readiness for the next shot. The magazine is in the butt and is loaded by a clip from the top of the frame, with the slide to the rear. The Steyr Model 1911 was taken into service by the Austro-Hungarian Army in 1912 – the cavalry, however, continuing to use the Roth-Steyr Model 1907 (see note on page 120, right) – and was also used by the Romanian Army in World War I. It was in Austrian service for many years, although manufacture of the pistol ended in 1918.

Belgium
**BROWNING MODEL 1900**

| | |
|---|---|
| **Length:** | 6·75" (171mm) |
| **Weight:** | 22oz (·62kg) |
| **Barrel:** | 4" (102mm) |
| **Calibre:** | 7·65mm |
| **Rifling:** | 6 groove, r/hand |
| **Capacity:** | Seven |
| **Muz Vel:** | c940 f/s (287 m/s) |
| **Sights:** | Fixed |

Argentina
**HAFDASA SELF-LOADING PISTOL**

| | |
|---|---|
| **Length:** | 9" (229mm) |
| **Weight:** | 39oz (1·1kg) |
| **Barrel:** | 5" (127mm) |
| **Calibre:** | ·45" |
| **Rifling:** | 6 groove, r/hand |
| **Capacity:** | Seven |
| **Muz Vel:** | c860 f/s (262 m/s) |
| **Sights:** | Fixed |

Belgium
**BROWNING MODEL 1900**
The figure "1948", clearly visible on the frame of this pistol, is the arm's number, not its date of manufacture, and shows that it must be from one of the earliest batches to have been produced.

Argentina
**HAFDASA SELF-LOADING PISTOL**
At first sight this pistol might be mistaken for a Colt 1911—but note the absence of a grip safety and the fact that the finger-grips on the slide are grooved in groups of three, and not evenly spaced

United States of America
**COLT MODEL 1911**

| | |
|---|---|
| **Length:** | 8·5" (216mm) |
| **Weight:** | 39oz (1·1kg) |
| **Barrel:** | 5" (127mm) |
| **Calibre:** | ·455" |
| **Rifling:** | 6 groove, l/hand |
| **Capacity:** | Seven |
| **Muz Vel:** | c860 f/s (262 m/s) |
| **Sights:** | Fixed |

United States of America
**COLT REMINGTON MODEL 1911A1**

| | |
|---|---|
| **Length:** | 8·5" (216mm) |
| **Weight:** | 39oz (1·1kg) |
| **Barrel:** | 5" (127mm) |
| **Calibre:** | ·45" |
| **Rifling:** | 6 groove, l/hand |
| **Capacity:** | Seven |
| **Muz Vel:** | c860 f/s (262 m/s) |
| **Sights:** | Fixed |

United States of America
**COLT MODEL 1911**
One of the most famous of all self-loading pistols, designed by John M. Browning, the Colt Model 1911 is seen here in the ·455in calibre version made for use by Canadian forces during World War I.

United States of America
**COLT REMINGTON MODEL 1911A1**
External differences between the Model 1911 and 1911A1 include the latter's slightly shorter hammer, longer horn on the grip safety, and the chamfering away of arc-shaped grooves behind the trigger.

Belgium
## BROWNING MODEL 1900

A weapon similar to the pistol seen here is illustrated on page 107 (top). This example, however, has some slight variations, and since something is also known of its personal history it has been judged worthy of inclusion. This model was the first of a long series of self-loading pistols to be made by Fabrique Nationale of Belgium to the designs of the famous American John M. Browning, and it is frequently referred to as the "Old Model". It fires a cartridge originally specially-designed by Browning for use in this particular model; the same round is now widely used in numerous other self-loading pistols. The magazine, which fits into the butt, is here shown separately; it will be noted that parts of the zig-zag magazine spring are just visible through the perforations. The pistol is numbered (*not* dated) "1948" and thus must be from one of the very earliest batches produced. After 10.000 of these arms had been made, subsequent examples had a lanyard ring fitted to the frame. The original design on the butt-plate incorporated a replica of the weapon and the words "F.N."; on later examples the pistol was omitted. This particular specimen has been fitted at some time with non-regulation aluminium grips. In spite of its age, it still works perfectly: it is known to have been carried as a private weapon by a French infantry officer during the Algerian Insurrection of 1954-62. A pistol of this type was used by the student Gavrilo Princip, who assassinated the Archduke Ferdinand and his wife at Sarajevo in June, 1914.

Argentina
## HAFDASA SELF-LOADING PISTOL

The name of this pistol is taken from the initials of the Argentinian firm which made it: Hispano-Argentine Fabricas De Automobiles SA, of Buenos Aires. The firm began making self-loading pistols of Colt 1911 type for the Argentinian Government in the 1930s, and the arm illustrated here is one such. At first sight it might be taken for a Colt, but the absence of a grip safety and the fact that the finger-grips on the slide are grooved in groups of three, as opposed to the even spacing of those on the Colt, make it clear that it is not. It is however, mechanically identical to the Colt. The weapon appears to be of sound construction and it has been made in large numbers: it is used extensively by the Argentinian Army, Police and other authorities, and some were bought by Great Britain for use in World War II. The left-hand side of the receiver bears the legend: "PISTOLA AUTOMATICA CAL 45 FABRICADA POR 'HAFDASA'. PATENTES INTERNACIONALES 'BALLESTER-MOLINA' INDUSTRIA ARGENTINA". The fame of the Colt 1911 made it inevitable that it would be widely copied.

United States of America
## COLT MODEL 1911

Although there was at first little interest in self-loading pistols in the United States, the firm of Colt soon realized that there was to be a future for weapons of the type. By 1898, Colt had produced a prototype which went into limited production as the Model 1900. It was based on the action invented by John M. Browning and was a limited success only. However, the firm persevered and in the next few years produced an entire series of new types which reached culmination in the most famous of all, the Model 1911. The arm was designed by Browning, and right from its inception was intended to be a service weapon. The United States Army tested it exhaustively for several years and finally decided on its adoption as the standard service weapon. The pistol still holds that position at the present time. It has, of course, been to some extent altered and improved, mostly in its earlier years; in 1921, it was redesignated the 1911A1. The example illustrated here was made for use by Canadian forces in World War I, hence its calibre.

**Below:** *An American soldier armed with a Colt Model 1911 pistol during the Korean War.*

United States of America
## COLT REMINGTON MODEL 1911A1

Because of the great demand for the Model 1911, Colt subcontracted to other reputable American firms: the arm on page 123 (bottom) was made by Remington for US forces in World War II. This Model 1911A1 incorporates improvements over the Colt Model 1911, including a longer horn on the grip safety; a slightly shorter hammer; and the chamfering away of arc-shaped grooves behind the trigger—as well as internal differences. But in spite of these, it remains fundamentally the same arm. It consists of three main parts: the receiver; the barrel; and the slide, which works on ribs machined on to the receiver. When the slide is fully forward, the barrel is locked to it by means of lugs on the barrel's upper surface, which engage in slots in the slide. When the slide is forced to the rear—either manually for initial loading or by the cartridges after the first shot—the barrel moves only a very short distance before its rear end drops, disengaging it from the slide which thereafter continues to the rear.

**Below:** *A US infantryman in Europe, January 1944, with a Colt Remington Model 1911A1.*

Soviet Union
**TULA-TOKAREV 1930**

| | |
|---|---|
| **Length:** | 7·7" (196mm) |
| **Weight:** | 29oz (·82kg) |
| **Barrel:** | 4·6" (117mm) |
| **Calibre:** | 7·62mm |
| **Rifling:** | 4 groove, l/hand |
| **Capacity:** | Eight |
| **Muz Vel:** | c1350 f/s (411 m/s) |
| **Sights:** | Fixed |

Spain
**LLAMA SELF-LOADING PISTOL**

| | |
|---|---|
| **Length:** | 9·5" (241mm) |
| **Weight:** | 40oz (1·13kg) |
| **Barrel:** | 5" (127mm) |
| **Calibre:** | 9mm |
| **Rifling:** | 6 groove, l/hand |
| **Capacity:** | Seven |
| **Muz Vel:** | c850 f/s (259 m/s) |
| **Sights:** | Fixed |

Soviet Union
**TULA-TOKAREV 1930**
This Soviet pistol appears at first glance to be of hammerless type. In fact, much of the hammer is concealed within the frame; only the cogwheel-type hammer-comb is visible, just behind the backsight.

Spain
**LLAMA SELF-LOADING PISTOL**
Unlike the Colt Model 1911, on which it is very closely based, this Spanish pistol has no grip safety; it is fitted with an orthodox safety catch on the left side of the frame, below the hammer.

Poland
**RADOM VIS-35**

| | |
|---|---|
| **Length:** | 8·3" (211mm) |
| **Weight:** | 37oz (1·05kg) |
| **Barrel:** | 4·5" (114mm) |
| **Calibre:** | 9mm |
| **Rifling:** | 6 groove, r/hand |
| **Capacity:** | Eight |
| **Muz Vel:** | c1150 f/s (351 m/s) |
| **Sights:** | Fixed |

Spain
**ECHEVERRIA STAR MODEL B**

| | |
|---|---|
| **Length:** | 8" (203mm) |
| **Weight:** | 34oz (·96kg) |
| **Barrel:** | 5" (127mm) |
| **Calibre:** | 9mm |
| **Rifling:** | 4 groove, r/hand |
| **Capacity:** | Eight |
| **Muz Vel:** | c1100 f/s (335 m/s) |
| **Sights:** | Fixed |

Poland
**RADOM VIS-35**
As well as a grip safety, the Radom incorporates a device (activated by the lever below the back-sight) for retracting the firing-pin, so that it may be carried safely with the hammer down on a round.

Spain
**ECHEVERRIA STAR MODEL B**
This pistol, in current use by the Spanish armed forces, is another of the many arms based on the Colt Model 1911 and its variants. It is designed to use the powerful 9mm Parabellum cartridge.

Soviet Union
## TULA-TOKAREV 1930

This official Russian Government pistol takes the first part of its designation from the state arsenal where it was made and the second part from Feodor Tokarev, a well-known Russian designer from the 1920s onward. It is mechanically a copy of various Colt-Browning types, with one or two modifications to simplify production, and one or two actual improvements in design. In the original version, the barrel locking lugs were machined on to the barrel's upper surface, but for ease of manufacture the lugs were replaced in 1933 by bands which went completely round the barrel. This involved no mechanical changes. On a pistol of this type, the magazine has no lips, a cartridge guide being incorporated into the frame. This is an improvement, for the thin metal of a magazine can become distorted relatively easily. At first sight, it might be thought that this weapon is of hammerless type; in fact, much of the hammer is concealed within the frame. The Tula-Tokarev has no safety catch, but the hammer may be placed at half-cock.

*In heroic pose, a soldier of the Red Army brandishes a 7·62mm Tula-Tokarev self-loading pistol.*

Spain
## LLAMA SELF-LOADING PISTOL

The great success and wide acceptance of the Colt Model 1911 self-loading pistol and its successive variations made it inevitable that the arm should become the subject of extensive copying. In this field Spanish manufacturers were particularly active. The Spanish firm of Gabilondo y Urresti was originally formed at Guernica in 1904. After the end of World War I, the firm moved to Elgoibar, near Eibar, and began to make pistols under the name of Gabilondo y Cia. In 1931, the firm began to manufacture a new range of Colt-type pistols under the general trade name of "Llama", and these arms have continued in production until the present day. They are, in general, very well-made and reliable weapons and sell in considerable quantities. They have been produced in a wide variety of models and calibres—some of blowback type, some with locked breeches, and yet others with grip safeties—so that individual models are not always easy to identify. The pistol illustrated here appears to be a model produced in *c*1939. Its general style, which very closely resembles that of the Colt, is clear from the photograph. It is designed to fire the ·38in Colt Super cartridge—a very powerful round, and one which, of course, necessitates a locked breech. This pistol has no grip safety but is fitted with an orthodox safety catch on the left, below the hammer. Since 1931, more than 15 differentiated models in the Llama series have been made by Gabilondo y Cia, in calibres varying from 9mm (like that on page 126) to ·22in Short.

Poland
**RADOM VIS-35**

The Radom Arms Factory of Poland was set up soon after the end of World War I. It was initially intended principally for the production of military rifles, a few revolvers also being made, but soon after 1930 it was decided that the Polish Army required a self-loading pistol. After the consideration of various designs, an indigenous model was finally adopted, and by 1935 the VIS, illustrated here, was in extensive production. Like most later self-loading pistols, it is based more or less closely on the basic designs of the American John M. Browning, with some relatively minor changes either for ease of manufacture or in the shape of actual improvements incorporated in the light of experience. The pistol works in the orthodox way: lugs on the upper surface of the barrel engage corresponding slots in the slide when it is locked; the barrel recoils briefly and then drops to disengage when the slide is either drawn to the rear manually or blown back by the gases produced by the explosion of the cartridge. As may be seen, the weapon has a grip safety at the rear of the butt. No manual safety as such is fitted, but the arm incorporates a device for retracting the firing pin, and this allows it to be carried safely with a round in the chamber and the hammer down. This device is activated by the lever below the backsight; the action of cocking the hammer manually returns the firing pin to its proper position. The markings on the left side of the slide, which include the Polish eagle, are clearly visible.

Spain
**ECHEVERRIA STAR MODEL B**

This arm is another of the Spanish self-loading pistols based more or less closely on the Colt Model 1911 and its variants. The firm of Echeverria came into existence in about 1908 in Eibar, and although its later history is somewhat obscure, it appears to have been making self-loading pistols of one kind or another ever since. It has also made submachine guns of various types from time to time. The trade name of "Star" was adopted in 1919 and has been in use ever since on a quite bewildering variety of pistols of various types, sizes, calibres and systems of numbering and classification. The pistol illustrated here is a Star Model B, introduced in about 1928. It is fairly closely based on the Colt, but lacks the grip safety peculiar to that arm. It is a robust and well-made weapon, and since it is chambered for the powerful 9mm Parabellum cartridge it necessarily fires from a locked breech. This works on the well-known Browning principle: after a brief period of recoil, the rear end of the barrel drops, thus unlocking itself from the interior of the slide, which continues to the rear and cocks the hammer. Having done so, it comes forward, chambers the next cartridge, and relocks the breech in readiness for the next shot. Towards the end of World War II, the Star Model B (and Models A, M and P) was re-designed, with a dismantling catch on the right of the frame, and designated the "Super Star". In 1946 it was adopted as the standard pistol of the Spanish Army, replacing the Unceta Astra 400 (see page 147, bottom).

Germany
**LUGER PARABELLUM MODEL 1908 (P08)**

| | |
|---|---|
| **Length:** | 8·75" (222mm) |
| **Weight:** | 30oz (·85kg) |
| **Barrel:** | 4" (102mm) |
| **Calibre:** | 9mm |
| **Rifling:** | 8 groove, r/hand |
| **Capacity:** | Eight |
| **Muz Vel:** | c1150 f/s (351 m/s) |
| **Sights:** | Fixed |

Czechoslovakia
**CESKA ZBROJOVKA MODEL 39**

| | |
|---|---|
| **Length:** | 8·1" (206mm) |
| **Weight:** | 33oz (·94kg) |
| **Barrel:** | 4·65" (118mm) |
| **Calibre:** | 9mm |
| **Rifling:** | 6 groove, r/hand |
| **Capacity:** | Eight |
| **Muz Vel:** | c950 f/s (290 m/s) |
| **Sights:** | Fixed |

Germany
**LUGER PARABELLUM MODEL 1908 (P08)**
The Luger was basically similar to the Borchardt (see pages 98-99, bottom), the design having been modified and improved by Georg Luger. This famous pistol was in production from 1908 to 1943.

Czechoslovakia
**CESKA ZBROJOVKA MODEL 39**
Although well-made, the CZ Model 39 was not a successful military arm. Its cartridge was underpowered, and the fact that it could be fired only by a quite heavy trigger-pull made for inaccuracy.

Germany
**WALTHER P38**

| | |
|---|---|
| **Length:** | 8·4" (213mm) |
| **Weight:** | 34oz (·96kg) |
| **Barrel:** | 5" (127mm) |
| **Calibre:** | 9mm |
| **Rifling:** | 6 groove, r/hand |
| **Capacity:** | Eight |
| **Muz Vel:** | c1150 f/s (351 m/s) |
| **Sights:** | Fixed |

Germany
**LUGER 08/20**

| | |
|---|---|
| **Length:** | 8·75" (222mm) |
| **Weight:** | 30oz (·85kg) |
| **Barrel:** | 3·75" (95mm) |
| **Calibre:** | 7·65mm |
| **Rifling:** | 8 groove, r/hand |
| **Capacity:** | Eight |
| **Muz Vel:** | c1150 f/s (351 m/s) |
| **Sights:** | Fixed |

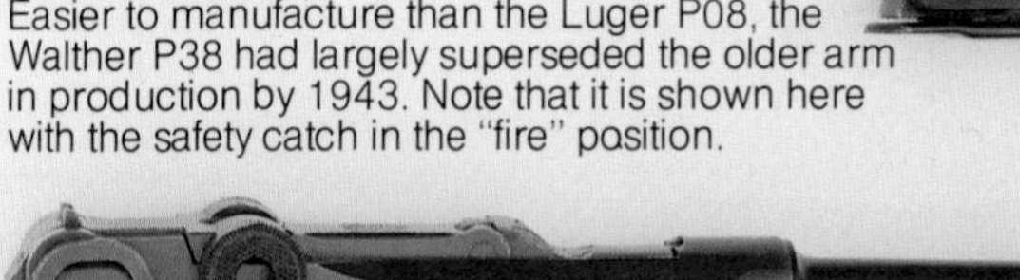

Germany
**WALTHER P38**
Easier to manufacture than the Luger P08, the Walther P38 had largely superseded the older arm in production by 1943. Note that it is shown here with the safety catch in the "fire" position.

Germany
**LUGER 08/20**
This Luger embodies two measures adopted by German manufacturers to circumvent Treaty restrictions: a barrel less than 4in (102mm) in length—and a 9mm barrel blank bored for a 7·65mm round.

Germany
## LUGER PARABELLUM MODEL 1908 (P08)

The Luger pistol—basically a Borchardt modified and improved by Luger—appeared at the end of the 19th century. It was manufactured by the Deutsche Waffen und Munitionsfabrik (DWM) of Berlin. The pistol illustrated went into production in 1908 and was almost immediately adopted by the German Army, which was seeking a self-loader to replace its revolver. This assured the arm's success, as many smaller countries followed Germany's lead and purchased large numbers of Lugers for their armed forces. It served the Germans well during World War I and, like the Mauser, became something of a household word, establishing a popular reputation which is, perhaps, greater than its real merit. After World War I, its manufacture was taken over by Mauser, who continued to make both military and civilian models. This particular example is one of those made by Mauser and is dated "1940". In 1938 the German Army adopted the Walther P38, but Lugers were in production until 1943.

Czechoslovakia
## CESKA ZBROJOVKA MODEL 39

An arms manufactory was established at Pilsen in Czechoslovakia, then a newly-founded country in 1919, and moved to Strakonitz in 1921. It made a wide variety of weapons and accessories for the Czech Army. Between the two World Wars, before Czechoslovakia came under Communist control, the company produced both pocket arms and service-type pistols. The earliest of these fired from a locked breech, but as the short cartridge employed hardly warranted the use of this system, subsequent models reverted to simple blowback. The Ceská Zbrojovka Model 39 pistol illustrated here is very well made and finished, but it was not a success as a military arm. In spite of its weight and bulk, it fires only a low-powered round, and its exposed hammer cannot be cocked: the arm must be fired by a quite heavy pull on the trigger, and this, of course, hardly contributes to its accuracy. It is very easy to strip: forward pressure on a milled catch on the left of the frame allows the slide and barrel to be raised on a rear hinge.

**Left:** *A German soldier during the Russian campaign, armed with a Luger P08 pistol.*

Germany
## WALTHER P38

In the early 1930s, the Carl Walther Waffenfabrik developed two prototype military pistols, the AP (hammerless) and HP (external hammer). The German military chose the latter. By 1943 the P38 had largely superseded the Luger 08. The P38's cartridge made it necessary to employ a locked breech. The lower part of the barrel incorporates a separate locking block, the lugs of which engage in recesses in the slide when the pistol is ready to be fired. When a cartridge is fired, the barrel and slide recoil briefly together, until the lugs are carried out of the slide; then the barrel stops, allowing the slide to continue to the rear to cock the hammer. The slide then travels forward under the pressure of the recoil spring, to continue the cycle by pushing another cartridge into the chamber. The only actions necessary to fire the loaded pistol, therefore, are to push up the safety catch with the thumb to the "fire" position (the position which is shown in the colour photograph) and then press the trigger.

**Below:** *A German guarding US prisoners in the Ardennes carries a 9mm Walther P38.*

Germany
## LUGER 08/20

After World War I, Germany was largely disarmed and severe restrictions were placed on arms production. However, some degree of manufacture for export was later permitted, and since vast stocks of components were still hidden away in various places a good deal of cannibalization was then carried out. The original title of "Parabellum" for DWM's Model 1908 had by then largely given way to that of "Luger". The demand for this arm was considerable—partly for use and partly because it was a popular souvenir. The pistol illustrated here appears to be one of the post-1918 arms put together by DWM, whose monogram appears on the toggle joint. One way of circumventing the restrictions imposed by the Treaty of Versailles, which laid down that all weapons made must be of less than 9mm calibre, was to bore 9mm barrel blanks for smaller-calibre rounds. Another was to make the barrels marginally shorter than the maximum of 4in (102mm) specified by the Treaty. Both are used here.

**Below:** *British paratrooper captured at Arnhem, guarded by a soldier with a Luger 08/20.*

Italy
### BERETTA MODEL 1934

| | |
|---|---|
| **Length:** | 6" (152mm) |
| **Weight:** | 23oz (·65kg) |
| **Barrel:** | 3·75" (95mm) |
| **Calibre:** | 9mm |
| **Rifling:** | 4 groove, r/hand |
| **Capacity:** | Nine |
| **Muz Vel:** | c750 f/s (229 m/s) |
| **Sights:** | Fixed |

Italy
### BERETTA MODEL 1935

| | |
|---|---|
| **Length:** | 6" (152mm) |
| **Weight:** | 23oz (·65kg) |
| **Barrel:** | 3·75" (95mm) |
| **Calibre:** | 7·65mm |
| **Rifling:** | 4 groove, r/hand |
| **Capacity:** | Seven |
| **Muz Vel:** | c800 f/s (244 m/s) |
| **Sights:** | Fixed |

Italy
**BERETTA MODEL 1934**
Many British officers acquired these pistols during World War II —only to find that, being intended to take the 9mm Short cartridge, they would not fire standard 9mm Parabellum Sten Gun ammunition.

Italy
**BERETTA MODEL 1935**
This Beretta Model 1935 is fitted with a spur-shaped extension below the magazine, offering added support for the little finger of the firer's hand.

United States of America
**REMINGTON MODEL 51**

| | |
|---|---|
| **Length:** | 6·5" (165mm) |
| **Weight:** | 21oz (·6kg) |
| **Barrel:** | 3·5" (89mm) |
| **Calibre:** | ·38" |
| **Rifling:** | 7 groove, r/hand |
| **Capacity:** | Seven |
| **Muz Vel:** | c900 f/s (274 m/s) |
| **Sights:** | Fixed |

France
**MAB MODEL D**

| | |
|---|---|
| **Length:** | 5·8" (147mm) |
| **Weight:** | 26oz (·74kg) |
| **Barrel:** | 3·2" (81mm) |
| **Calibre:** | 7·65mm |
| **Rifling:** | 7 groove, r/hand |
| **Capacity:** | Nine |
| **Muz Vel:** | c800 f/s (244 m/s) |
| **Sights:** | Fixed |

United States of America
**REMINGTON MODEL 51**
This is the ·38in Auto calibre model—by far the more common—of the Pedersen-designed pistol, appearing in 1919, which was also made in ·32in calibre. Note the grip safety at the back of the butt.

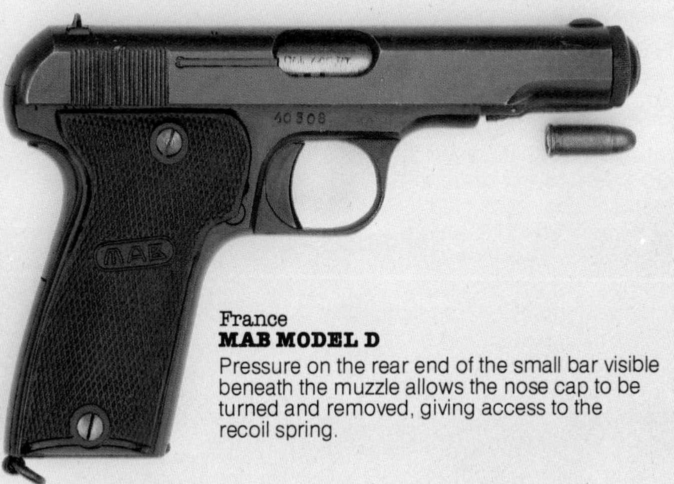


France
**MAB MODEL D**
Pressure on the rear end of the small bar visible beneath the muzzle allows the nose cap to be turned and removed, giving access to the recoil spring.

Italy
## BERETTA MODEL 1934

The Beretta company of Brescia has now been in existence for 300 years, during which time it has established a very well-deserved reputation for the excellence of its products. It originally confined its activities to sporting guns and rifles: it was not until the early years of World War I that the company of necessity turned to the manufacture of military weapons of all kinds, including self-loading pistols. The first Beretta self-loader, the Model 1915, was of wartime quality and was designed to take a 7·65mm cartridge; this was soon replaced by a version in 9mm calibre, which was considered more suitable for service use. Development continued after World War I, with a steady improvement in design until 1934, when the weapon illustrated here appeared. Like its predecessors, the Model 1934 works by simple blowback action: thus, although it is of 9mm calibre, it fires a short cartridge in order to keep the gas pressure within safe limits. As may be seen, it has an external hammer: this may be cocked either by the rearward movement of the slide, or manually, and it has a half-cock position. Most examples of the Model 1934 were fitted with a curved lower extension to the magazine (see the arm illustrated below), so as to ensure a firm grip for a user with a large hand, but some (like the example seen here) were fitted with plain magazines. This arm became the standard Italian service pistol in 1935: this particular example is marked with the letters "RE" surmounted by a crown, indicating that it is a military model.

Italy
## BERETTA MODEL 1935

The Beretta Model 1934 was so successful that in the following year the Beretta company produced the Model 1935. It was very similar in all essentials to the earlier weapon, but was of the smaller calibre of 7·65mm. The specimen illustrated is fitted with a spur-shaped extension below the magazine to offer added support for the little finger of the firer's hand. Like the Model 1934, it has a safety catch on the left side of the frame and is usually fitted with a loop for a lanyard on the lower part of the butt. The Model 1935 was extensively issued to the Italian Navy and Air Force and was also used by the Italian police: the specimen illustrated bears the initials "PS" *(Publica Sicurreza)*, indicating that it is a police weapon. Like most Berettas of the period, this arm bears details of the calibre on the left side of the slide, which is also dated "1941"; the date is followed by the Roman numerals "XIX", its date in the Fascist Calendar of 1922.

*The Beretta Model 1934—this specimen bears the cypher of the Duke of Aosta—was similar in all essentials to the Model 1935, but of 9mm calibre. Note spur extension on magazine*

United States of America
## REMINGTON MODEL 51

The Remington Arms Company was founded by Eliphalet Remington in 1816 and thereafter produced a considerable range of rifles, revolvers, pistols and shotguns. Some of its earlier hand guns are described in the section of this book devoted to percussion revolvers and cartridge revolvers. Remington's first entry into the field of self-loading pistols occurred in 1917, when the company received a contract to manufacture Model 1911 Colts, but this contract was terminated in 1918, at the end of World War I. However, the company had plans for a self-loading pistol of its own, based on the designs of J. D. Pedersen, a well-known and well-respected figure in the world of small arms. This weapon appeared on the market in 1919 as the Model 51. It was made in two calibres—·38in Auto (the arm illustrated here) and, in much smaller numbers, in ·32in. The mechanism is of the type known as delayed blowback. When the cartridge is fired, the slide and its internal breech-block recoil briefly together; the block then stops, allowing the slide to continue to the rear, but after a brief pause the block is released and rejoins the slide. Both then come forward under the influence of the recoil spring, which is fitted round the fixed barrel. The weapon is fitted with a grip safety (visible at the back of the butt) and also has a normal safety at the rear left end of the frame. The Remington Model 51 was an excellent weapon but, because it was expensive to produce—and thus had to be priced accordingly—it never gained the popularity it deserved.

France
## MAB MODEL D

The initials MAB stand for the Manufacture d'Armes de Bayonne, a company which, since 1921, has been chiefly concerned with the manufacture of self-loading pistols of pocket type. The company's products are well made, but most of them are based on the designs of others: the weapon illustrated here, for example, bears a considerable resemblance to the Browning. It was first put on the market in 1933 as the Model C but, enlarged and with a better-shaped butt, reappeared as the Model D—under which designation it is still in production. It is of simple blowback design: when the cartridge is fired, the slide and block are forced to the rear, compressing the coil spring which is located round the barrel. The subsequent forward movement strips a round from the magazine and chambers it ready for the next shot. Access to the recoil spring is obtained by pressing up the rear end of the small bar visible under the muzzle: the nose cap can then be turned and removed, taking the spring with it.

*This French Resistance woman talking with Allied paratroopers in August 1944 has what looks to be a 7·65mm MAB pistol.*

Germany
**WALTHER PPK**

| | |
|---|---|
| **Length:** | 5·8" (147mm) |
| **Weight:** | 20oz (·57kg) |
| **Barrel:** | 3·15" (80mm) |
| **Calibre:** | 7·65mm |
| **Rifling:** | 6 groove, r/hand |
| **Capacity:** | Seven |
| **Muz Vel:** | c1000 f/s (305 m/s) |
| **Sights:** | Fixed |

Germany
**SAUER MODEL 38H**

| | |
|---|---|
| **Length:** | 6·75" (171mm) |
| **Weight:** | 25oz (·71kg) |
| **Barrel:** | 3·25" (83mm) |
| **Calibre:** | 7·65mm |
| **Rifling:** | 4 groove, r/hand |
| **Capacity:** | Eight |
| **Muz Vel:** | c900 f/s (274 m/s) |
| **Sights:** | Fixed |

Germany
**WALTHER PPK**
The PPK has an external hammer activated by a double-action lock; thus, it can be carried safely with the hammer down on a round, and fired simply by releasing the safety and pressing the trigger.

Germany
**SAUER MODEL 38H**
The internal hammer can be lowered by pressing the trigger while thumb-pressure allows the milled catch behind it to rise slowly. The pistol may then be re-cocked, if required, by depressing the catch.

Hungary
**FEGYVERGYAR MODEL 1937**

| | |
|---|---|
| **Length:** | 7·2" (183mm) |
| **Weight:** | 27oz (·76kg) |
| **Barrel:** | 4·33" (110mm) |
| **Calibre:** | 9mm |
| **Rifling:** | 6 groove, r/hand |
| **Capacity:** | Seven |
| **Muz Vel:** | c900 f/s (274 m/s) |
| **Sights:** | Fixed |

Germany
**WALTHER PP**

| | |
|---|---|
| **Length:** | 6·4" (163mm) |
| **Weight:** | 25oz (·71kg) |
| **Barrel:** | 3·8" (97mm) |
| **Calibre:** | 7·65mm |
| **Rifling:** | 6 groove, r/hand |
| **Capacity:** | Eight |
| **Muz Vel:** | c1000 f/s (305 m/s) |
| **Sights:** | Fixed |

Hungary
**FEGYVERGYAR MODEL 1937**
This is the original version of the Model 1937, firing a 9mm short cartridge. Pistols made under contract for Germany in 1943 were of 7·65mm calibre; they incorporated an orthodox safety catch, rather than the grip safety seen here.

Germany
**WALTHER PP**
The Walther PP (*P*olizei *P*istole; it was made primarily for police work) was used as a holster arm by many European police forces and was the Luftwaffe's standard pistol in World War II.

Germany
## WALTHER PPK

The famous German firm known as the Carl Walther Waffenfabrik was established in 1886, but it did not begin to make self-loading pistols until 1908. Its first nine models were numbered, but in 1929 it produced a tenth model designed specifically for police work, and this was designated the *Polizei Pistole* or "PP". This weapon (an example is illustrated on the previous page, below) was immediately popular, and two years later a smaller version was made for concealed use. It was intended for plain-clothes police work and was known as the "PPK": the "K", it was said, stood for *Kriminal*—itself short for *Kriminal Polizei,* the name of the German detective branch. The Walther PPK pistol, illustrated here, is of blowback type and it has several interesting and important features. The most notable, perhaps, is that it is provided with an external hammer activated by a double-action lock; this allows the pistol to be carried safely with a round in the chamber and the hammer down. Thus, all that is necessary to bring it into action is to push off the safety catch and press the trigger. It also has an indicator pin which protrudes through the top of the slide when there is a cartridge in the chamber—a very useful feature in any self-loading pistol, where the rounds cannot be seen as they can in a revolver. The earliest versions of this pistol had complete butt-frames with a pair of grips, but later examples had a front strap only, with a one-piece, moulded, wrap-round, plastic grip. Most also had a plastic extension on the bottom of the magazine, to increase the area of grip.

Germany
## SAUER MODEL 38H

The German firm of J. P. Sauer & Sohn is an old one, with a reputation for producing high-quality weapons. At first, its products were mainly sporting guns and rifles, but the company began to make self-loading pistols in 1913 and continued to do so until after World War II, when it turned to revolvers. The weapon illustrated here is one of Sauer's best products. It was first put on the market in 1938 (hence its Model number), but the outbreak of war soon afterwards restricted its use to German forces—and for some reason manufacture was not resumed afterwards. It works on the blowback principle, having a fixed barrel and an overall slide with the breech-block inside it. It has an internal hammer (hence the "H"—for *Hahn,* hammer—in the Model designation). The first round is chambered in the usual way by the manual operation of the slide, which also cocks the hammer, but thereafter there are various options. If required, the hammer may be lowered by pressing the trigger, with the thumb on the milled catch behind it, and allowing the catch to rise slowly. To fire after this procedure, the pistol can either be cocked by depressing the catch with the thumb, or fired double-action by pressing the trigger. Since World War II, the name of Sauer is best known in conjunction with that of Schweizerische Industrie Gesellschaft (SIG). SIG's exports are strictly limited by the Swiss government, so its designs are manufactured and exported by Sauer in Germany. Sauer alone makes a range of Colt-replica revolvers for the American market.

Hungary
## FEGYVERGYAR MODEL 1937

The Hungarian firm of Fegyvergyar (Fegyver es Gepgyar Reszvenytarsasag) was established at Budapest in the 19th century and gained a reputation for producing good-quality weapons. Its first self-loading pistol appeared in 1903, and there was a variety of later models, including a Hungarian Army pistol. The arm illustrated in colour on page 139 (top), the Fegyvergyar Model 1937, was the last of the series and went into production in the year after the death of its designer, Rudolf Frommer, who had been the firm's manager for some 35 years. It was quickly adopted by the Hungarian Army. It is a blowback type with a fixed barrel and an overall slide; the recoil spring is situated on a rod below the barrel. The first round is chambered in the normal way by the manual operation of the slide, which also cocks the external hammer. There is a spur on the magazine to extend the butt length. The original version was of 9mm calibre and fired a short cartridge suitable for a blowback pistol; its only safety device was its grip safety. In 1941, however, Germany took out a contract for a 7·65mm version and, apart from the first few made, these were all fitted with a safety catch of orthodox type on the left side of the frame. In this series, the original manufacturer's details on the slide were changed: the new markings were simply "P MOD 37 Kal 7·65", together with the manufacturer's code of "h.v." and the last two digits of the year of manufacture, which was 1943. Production reached around 85,000 and ended in 1944.

Germany
## WALTHER PP

This pistol, the Walther PP, may conveniently be described as the elder brother of the PPK (see left). It was of a new and, to some extent, revolutionary design, and rapidly achieved popularity after its appearance in 1929. As has already been stated, the weapon was made principally for police use, and the designation PP stands for *Polizei Pistole*. It was very soon adopted as a holster arm by several European police forces, and later also became the standard pistol of the German Luftwaffe. Its main feature was its double-action lock, which was basically of revolver type and which involved the use of an external hammer. A considerable risk is involved in carrying hammerless self-loaders—and even, to a lesser extent, many earlier hammer versions—with a round in the chamber. However, when a round has been loaded into the chamber of a Walther and the safety catch applied, the fall of the trigger may be disconcerting, but is completely safe, for the action of the safety places a steel guard between the hammer and the firing pin. The pistol is easily stripped by pulling down the trigger-guard and pushing very slightly to the left, after which the slide is eased off. In 1945 the Walther factory was badly damaged and the remains were removed by the Russians. The re-establishment of the firm at Ulm-am-Donau in the 1950s was facilitated by the continuing manufacture of the PP and PPK models under licence by the French firm of Manurhin. Apart from the manufacturer's markings, these French-made arms are identical to the originals.

France
**LE FRANÇAIS MODEL 28**

| | |
|---|---|
| **Length:** | 7·9" (201mm) |
| **Weight:** | 35oz (·99kg) |
| **Barrel:** | 5" (127mm) |
| **Calibre:** | 9mm |
| **Rifling:** | 6 groove, r/hand |
| **Capacity:** | Eight |
| **Muz Vel:** | c1100 f/s (335 m/s) |
| **Sights:** | Fixed |

France
**MAS MODEL 1950**

| | |
|---|---|
| **Length:** | 7·6" (193mm) |
| **Weight:** | 34oz (·96kg) |
| **Barrel:** | 4·3" (109mm) |
| **Calibre:** | 9mm |
| **Rifling:** | 4 groove, l/hand |
| **Capacity:** | Nine |
| **Muz Vel:** | c1100 f/s (335 m/s) |
| **Sights:** | Fixed |

France
**LE FRANÇAIS MODEL 28**
The magazine carries an extra round in its base. When the magazine has been pushed home, this round is withdrawn and placed in the breech; then the barrel hinge is closed and the arm is ready to fire.

France
**MAS MODEL 1950**
Firing the standard 9mm Parabellum cartridge, this was the first really satisfactory self-loader adopted by the French armed forces—earlier weapons having suffered from a lack of stopping-power.

Finland
**LAHTI L/35**

| | |
|---|---|
| **Length:** | 9·4" (239mm) |
| **Weight:** | 44oz (1·25kg) |
| **Barrel:** | 4·7" (119mm) |
| **Calibre:** | 9mm |
| **Rifling:** | 6 groove, r/hand |
| **Capacity:** | Eight |
| **Muz Vel:** | c1100 f/s (335 m/s) |
| **Sights:** | Fixed |

Czechoslovakia
**CESKA ZBROJOVKA CZ 1950**

| | |
|---|---|
| **Length:** | 8·2" (208mm) |
| **Weight:** | 34oz (·96kg) |
| **Barrel:** | 4·7" (119mm) |
| **Calibre:** | 7·62mm |
| **Rifling:** | 4 groove, r/hand |
| **Capacity:** | Eight |
| **Muz Vel:** | c1000 f/s (305 m/s) |
| **Sights:** | Fixed |

Finland
**LAHTI L/35**
This Lahti was made by Valtion, the Finnish state factory. Although it superficially resembles the Luger, the two are very different mechanically.

Czechoslovakia
**CESKA ZBROJOVKA CZ 1950**
The CZ 1950 is basically similar to the German Walther PP (see page 139, bottom). Like many European service arms, its cartridge lacked the stopping-power essential for service use.

France

## LE FRANÇAIS MODEL 28

The Manufacture Française d'Armes et Cycles de St Etienne dates from the mid-19th century, but only began to manufacture self-loading pistols just before World War I. These were small-calibre pocket arms—but in 1928 there appeared the Military Model, seen here. Its barrel is hinged at the front end—the pivot pin is visible in the photograph on the colour spread—and when a catch on the frame is pressed, the breech end rises clear of the slide, almost like a modern shotgun. As may be seen, the magazine carries an extra round in its base. When the magazine has been pushed home, this extra round is withdrawn and placed in the breech; then the barrel is closed and the pistol is ready to fire. When the magazine is withdrawn, the breech rises automatically: it is possible, in this model, to withdraw it partially and then load and fire single rounds, leaving the magazine's contents as a reserve. No extractor is fitted: the empty cases are blown clear by the residual gas pressure in the barrel after the shot has been fired. There is no locking system, the pistol functioning by blowback only—and it was probably this factor which doomed it, for the system meant that it must fire a cartridge too weak for service use. It may also happen that a misfired cartridge—admittedly a rare occurrence with modern ammunition—cannot be extracted without the use of some improvised tool. In spite of the eclipse of the Military Model, the smaller-calibre pocket arms produced by the company remained popular.

France

## MAS MODEL 1950

The initials that designate this arm are those of the Manufacture Nationale d'Armes de Saint Etienne, a French state factory. The revolvers originally used by the French armed forces (some of which have already been described) all suffered from the defect of firing weak cartridges. After the end of World War I, therefore, France decided to follow the example of virtually every other country on the European continent and change to a self-loading pistol. There followed a period of sporadic and somewhat leisurely experiment—at a time when another war was unthinkable—and it was not until 1935 that a self-loader was adopted. This, the MAS Model 1935, was a very sound and well-made weapon of basic Browning type—but it suffered from the same defect as the French revolvers: its 7·65mm round lacked stopping-power. After 1945, when France embarked on a major rearmament programme, one of the requirements was for a new pistol. The arm chosen was a re-designed Model 1935, capable of firing the standard 9mm Parabellum cartridge. This was a success and at last placed a really good pistol into the hands of French servicemen. The MAS Model 1950 was made both at Saint Etienne and the French state factory at Châtellerault, and although production has now ceased it is still in service with the French armed forces. The French Army has more recently adopted the 9mm MAB Model PA-15, a somewhat bulky delayed blowback arm with a butt specially enlarged to accommodate a fifteen-round magazine.

Finland
**LAHTI L/35**

Designed by Aimo Lahti and manufactured by Valtion, the Finnish state factory, this arm was originally planned in both 7·65mm and 9mm calibre, but the former remained a prototype. The Lahti became the official pistol of the Finnish armed forces in 1935; it gave good service in the Finnish campaign against the Russians in the early part of World War II, when it was found to be particularly reliable in very low temperatures. Although, as may be seen, it bears a general resemblance to the Luger, this is fortuitous: the two are quite different mechanically. The Lahti fires from a closed breech, the bolt being unlocked after a brief rearward travel and going on to complete the usual cycle. The mechanism incorporates a bolt accelerator —a curved arm which is so designed that it increases the rearward velocity of the bolt. A version of the Lahti was also used by the Swedish forces, by whom it was called the M/40.

*Finnish infantry in the war with Russia, 1939-40—when the L/35 was the standard pistol.*

Czechoslovakia
**CESKA ZBROJOVKA CZ 1950**

The firm of Ceska Zbrojovka was formed just after World War I. The self-loading pistol which is illustrated here, however, had its origins after the end of the World War II, when the Czech Army decided that it needed a new pistol. By 1950, the arm seen here was in production. It is basically similar to the German Walther PP (see page 139, below), although there are some manufacturing differences. It was a reasonably effective pistol but, like many European service arms, its calibre lacked the essential stopping-power for service use; therefore, within a very short period, it had been replaced as a military arm, although it continued in use for police purposes. It was replaced by the Ceska Zbrojovka CZ 1952 which, although of the same calibre, fired a much more powerful round from a locked breech, working by means of a roller device similar to that on the German MG 42 machine gun. This pistol was, in its turn, replaced by the Russian Makarov (page 151, bottom).

Italy
**GLISENTI 9mm 1910**

| | |
|---|---|
| **Length:** | 8·25" (210mm) |
| **Weight:** | 29oz (·82kg) |
| **Barrel:** | 3·9" (99mm) |
| **Calibre:** | 9mm |
| **Rifling:** | 6 groove, r/hand |
| **Capacity:** | Seven |
| **Muz Vel:** | c1000 f/s (305 m/s) |
| **Sights:** | Fixed |

Japan
**TAISHO 14 (14 NEN SHIKI KENJU)**

| | |
|---|---|
| **Length:** | 8·9" (226mm) |
| **Weight:** | 32oz (·91kg) |
| **Barrel:** | 4·75" (121mm) |
| **Calibre:** | 8mm |
| **Rifling:** | 6 groove, r/hand |
| **Capacity:** | Eight |
| **Muz Vel:** | c950 f/s (290 m/s) |
| **Sights:** | Fixed |

Italy
**GLISENTI 9mm 1910**
The milled screw prominent at the front of the frame of the Glisenti holds in position a plate covering much of the left side of the pistol. Its removal gives access to the working parts.

Japan
**TAISHO 14 (14 NEN SHIKI KENJU)**
An interesting feature of this Taisho 14 is the enlarged trigger-guard. This modification was introduced as a result of the Manchurian winter campaign of 1937, when gloves proved essential.

Japan
**TYPE 94**
**(94 SHIKI KENJU)**

| | |
|---|---|
| **Length:** | 7·1" (180mm) |
| **Weight:** | 28oz (·79kg) |
| **Barrel:** | 3·1" (79mm) |
| **Calibre:** | 8mm |
| **Rifling:** | 6 groove, r/hand |
| **Capacity:** | Six |
| **Muz Vel:** | c950 f/s (290 m/s) |
| **Sights:** | Fixed |

Spain
**UNCETA ASTRA 400**

| | |
|---|---|
| **Length:** | 9·25" (235mm) |
| **Weight:** | 38oz (1·08kg) |
| **Barrel:** | 5·5" (140mm) |
| **Calibre:** | 9mm |
| **Rifling:** | 6 groove, r/hand |
| **Capacity:** | Eight |
| **Muz Vel:** | c1100 f/s (335 m/s) |
| **Sights:** | Fixed |

Japan
**TYPE 94 (94 SHIKI KENJU)**
One of the worst service pistols ever made. The sear bar protrudes slightly from the left side of the frame when the weapon is cocked; thus, it may easily be discharged by an accidental blow.

Spain
**UNCETA ASTRA 400**
The Astra 400 was adopted by the Spanish Army in 1921, the year of its appearance. Although it fires a powerful 9mm cartridge, it works on straight blowback, without a breech-locking device.

Italy
## GLISENTI 9mm 1910

The Italian company at first called Real Fabbricca d'Armi Glisenti began operations in Brescia in c1889 and was responsible for the manufacture of the Bodeo Model 1889 Service revolver (see pages 68-70). After reorganization as Soc. Siderurgica Glisenti of Turin in the early 1900s its experiments with self-loading pistols culminated in the weapon illustrated, which is believed to have been based on a pistol made by two Belgian designers in 1905. The Glisenti was put into production in 1910 and was adopted by the Italian Army. The pistol fires from a locked breech. When the first shot is fired, barrel and bolt recoil briefly together. The barrel then stops in its rearward position, while the bolt, having unlocked itself, continues its travel. As it comes forward, it strips and chambers the next round and drives the barrel forward. As it does so, a wedge rises from the frame and locks the whole into position. The system is complex and not very strong; thus, the cartridge fired is less powerful than the Parabellum of comparable calibre. The pistol's trigger mechanism is peculiar: the striker is not cocked by the moving parts, but by a projection on the trigger; the striker is forced backwards against a spring until it trips and then comes forward to fire the round. This makes the trigger-pull very long. The milled screw at the front of the frame holds in position a plate covering much of the left side; its removal gives access to the working parts. Although it became obsolete in 1934, some were in service in World War II.

Japan
## TAISHO 14 (14 NEN SHIKI KENJU)

The first self-loading pistol officially adopted by the Japanese Army was the Nambu, which went through various modifications from 1909 onward. The weapon illustrated here represents the final modification; it first appeared in 1925 and remained in service until the end of World War II. When the pistol is fired, the barrel, bolt and receiver all recoil together for about ·2in (5mm). The movement of the barrel causes a block in the receiver to rotate, unlocking the bolt, which continues to the rear. The bolt is then impelled forward by two recoil springs, one on either side of it, and relocks for the round to be fired. The cocking-piece is circular; in early models, there are three grooves around it, but most of these pistols have the knurled type seen here. The magazine catch is a circular stud on the left of the frame, but there is also a small retaining spring in the front strap of the butt (the exterior part is visible in the photograph). An interesting feature of this arm is the enlarged trigger-guard.

*The 8mm Taisho 14 self-loading pistol of 1925 (right) is held next to an 8mm Nambu pistol.*

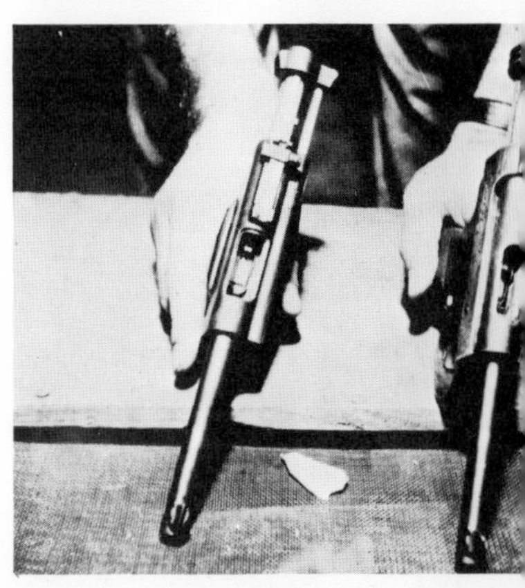

Japan

## TYPE 94 (94 SHIKI KENJU)

Until 1934, all self-loading pistols used by the Japanese services had been of the Nambu type shown on page 146 (below), but in that year a new and very different weapon was introduced. This weapon, the Type 94, illustrated here, takes its designation from the last two digits in the year of the Japanese calendar in which it was produced: 2594, corresponding to 1934 in the Christian calendar. The Type 94 was originally produced commercially, but the demands of the Sino-Japanese War led in 1937 to an increased need for arms, and the Japanese Government purchased this pistol in some quantities, mainly for Army tank crews and aircraft pilots. The weapon is cocked by pulling back the slide (which covers the entire top of the frame and barrel) by means of the milled ears visible at the rear. The breech is locked at the moment of firing by a vertically-moving slide which is cammed in and out of engagement by the brief recoil of the barrel. The trigger mechanism was most unreliable, particularly on later examples made during the course of World War II—when it was so eccentric as to be positively dangerous. The sear bar is exposed on the left-hand side of the frame; it protrudes slightly when the weapon is cocked, making it susceptible to accidental discharge by a blow. It was also possible for the pistol to be fired prematurely, before the breech was locked—and although the cartridge was low-powered, this was obviously a serious fault. This arm may probably be designated as one of the worst service pistols ever made.

Spain

## UNCETA ASTRA 400

The Spanish company of Unceta y Cia of Eibar and Guernica made self-loading pistols almost from the beginning of the 20th century. The firm's early products were mostly pocket pistols, but in 1921 it produced a heavier, service-type pistol of a different design. This was the Astra 400, a specimen of which is illustrated here; it was adopted by the Spanish Army in the same year as it appeared. The pistol has a stepped slide of tubular form: its front end envelops the barrel, while its rear end acts as breechblock. The recoil spring is positioned around the barrel and inside the slide, and is held in place by the bush visible at the muzzle. The pistol has an internal hammer and a grip safety. Probably the main point of interest is that although it fires a cartridge of considerable power, it works on straight blowback, without any form of breech-locking device. This is made possible by the use of a heavy slide and an unusually strong recoil spring, which between them reduce the backward action to within safe limits. This makes the pistol rather heavy and, in spite of the grooved finger-grips on its slide, it is quite hard to cock. Manufacture of the Astra 400 ceased in 1946, by which time more than 105,000 had been made (including a very few in 7·65mm calibre). The model and its variants gained wide acceptance. It was purchased by the French Army fairly soon after its introduction and the smaller Astra 300 (in 7·65mm and 9mm) and Astra 600 (9mm Parabellum) were both purchased for German service during World War II.

Belgium
**BROWNING 9mm Mk I***

| | |
|---|---|
| **Length:** | 7·75" (197mm) |
| **Weight:** | 35oz (·99kg) |
| **Barrel:** | 4·65" (118mm) |
| **Calibre:** | 9mm |
| **Rifling:** | 4 groove, r/hand |
| **Capacity:** | Thirteen |
| **Muz Vel:** | c1100 f/s (335 m/s) |
| **Sights:** | Fixed |

Belgium
**BROWNING 9mm Mk 1***
The stripped Browning below shows, top to bottom: slide; barrel; recoil spring (with slide locking lever to left); and main frame with hammer cocked.

Czechoslovakia
**CESKA ZBROJOVKA CZ 27**

| | |
|---|---|
| **Length:** | 6·25" (159mm) |
| **Weight:** | 25·5oz (·72kg) |
| **Barrel:** | 4" (102mm) |
| **Calibre:** | 7·65mm |
| **Rifling:** | 6 groove, r/hand |
| **Capacity:** | Eight |
| **Muz Vel:** | c900 f/s (274 m/s) |
| **Sights:** | Fixed |

Soviet Union
**MAKAROV 9mm**

| | |
|---|---|
| **Length:** | 6·35" (161mm) |
| **Weight:** | 25oz (·71kg) |
| **Barrel:** | 3·8" (97mm) |
| **Calibre:** | 9mm |
| **Rifling:** | 4 groove, r/hand |
| **Capacity:** | Eight |
| **Muz Vel:** | c1075 f/s (328 m/s) |
| **Sights:** | Fixed |

Czechoslovakia
**CESKA ZBROJOVKA CZ 27**
The CZ 27 may be distinguished from the near-identical CZ 24 by the fact that the finger-grooves at the rear of the slide are vertical rather than diagonal. More than 500,000 of these pistols were made.

Soviet Union
**MAKAROV 9mm**
When the last round in the magazine has been fired, the magazine follower rises far enough to push up the slide stop and hold the slide to the rear, indicating that re-loading is necessary.

Belgium

## BROWNING 9mm Mk I*

This is the last of Browning's pistol designs and was introduced in 1935, when it was taken into service by the Belgian Army. It was made in various versions, including one with an adjustable sight and a combined holster/stock of the type found on the original Mausers. When the Germans occupied Belgium in 1940, they continued the manufacture of these weapons—although it is said that various Belgian sabotage operations lowered the quality, sometimes to the point where the arms made were actually dangerous to use. A number of FN engineers went to Britain, taking the drawings with them. In 1942 these were sent to Canada, where the firm of John Inglis put the arms into production for Allied use; the weapon illustrated here is one of this series. After the war, manufacture reverted to the FN factory and the weapon was also put on sale commercially as the Hi-Power. It is currently in use by the British Army and other countries' services.

*This British sergeant during World War II is armed with a captured German-manufactured version of the 9mm Browning GP35 self-loading pistol. The same pistol was produced in Canada for Allied use as the Mk 1, Mk 1* and Mk 2.*

Czechoslovakia

## CESKA ZBROJOVKA CZ 27

The Ceska Zbrojovka factory was set up just after World War I, when the newly-formed country of Czechoslovakia began to establish the various industries needed by a modern state. Manufacture of self-loading pistols began immediately and still continues. In 1924 there appeared a military-type pistol firing a short 9mm cartridge from a locked breech. The designer, however, considered that a locking system was unnecessary for such a relatively low-powered round, and redesigned the pistol to eliminate this feature. The result was the CZ 27, illustrated on the colour spread (top right). Externally it appears to be almost identical to the 1924 model, the main apparent difference being that the finger-grooves at the rear of the slide are vertical rather than diagonal. The pistol works on straight blowback, with its recoil spring mounted around a rod situated below and parallel with the barrel. It has an external hammer and there is a magazine safety on the left-hand side of the frame, just above the magazine release stud. In pistols made before 1939, the milled top rib is marked "CESKA ZBROJOVKA AS v PRAZE", together with the serial number. When the Germans occupied Czechoslovakia, manufacture was continued on a considerable scale: weapons made during that period are recognizable by the fact that the inscription reads "BOHMISCHE WAFFEN FABRIK AG IN PRAG". The left side of the slide on this specimen is also marked "PISTOLE MODELL 27 KAL 7·65". Manufacture of this model continued until 1951.

Soviet Union

## MAKAROV 9mm

It is very difficult to obtain exact details of the development and production of Russian weapons, because of the almost impenetrable veil of secrecy which surrounds the affairs of all totalitarian regimes, but the following facts are believed to be correct. The Makarov pistol is thought to date from the early 1960s and is now the standard pistol for both the Soviet forces and for a variety of their satellites. Externally it is in almost every respect a copy of the German Walther PP (which is illustrated on page 139, bottom). However, there are some mechanical differences: by far the most important of these is the fact that the weapon has no locking system but fires on a simple blowback action. It is loaded in the orthodox way by inserting a magazine and operating the slide manually to chamber a round and cock the action. On firing, the slide is blown back by the rearward movement of the case. In order to avoid excessively stiff springs and heavy slides or breechblocks, the cartridge used is an intermediate one in terms of power, although apparently adequate. The pistol has an external hammer with a double-action lock; this means that it can be carried safely with a round in the chamber and the hammer down. There are slight differences between the pistols used by the various Soviet satellite countries, but none is really important. It is not clear why this new design was thought necessary at a time when at least one Soviet-bloc country (Hungary) already had a perfectly adequate self-loading pistol of this type: the 9mm PA-63, which is also based on the German Walther PP.

Italy
**BERETTA MODEL 81**

| | |
|---|---|
| **Length:** | 6·75" (171mm) |
| **Weight:** | 23·5oz (·67kg) |
| **Barrel:** | 3·75" (95mm) |
| **Calibre:** | 7·65mm |
| **Rifling:** | 6 groove, r/hand |
| **Capacity:** | Twelve |
| **Muz Vel:** | 985 f/s (300 m/s) |
| **Sights:** | Fixed |

The Beretta Model 84 pistol is stripped to its main components.

Italy
**BERETTA MODEL 81**
The Model 81—virtually indistinguishable from the Model 84, but taking a 7·65mm cartridge—is seen with its 12-round box magazine.

Italy
**BERETTA MODEL 92S**

| Length: | 8·5" (216mm) |
|---|---|
| Weight: | 35oz (·99kg) |
| Barrel: | 5" (127mm) |
| Calibre: | 9mm |
| Rifling: | 6 groove, r/hand |
| Capacity: | Thirteen |
| Muz Vel: | c1100 f/s (335 m/s) |
| Sights: | Fixed |

Italy
**BERETTA MODEL 84**

| Length: | 6·75" (171mm) |
|---|---|
| Weight: | 22oz (·62kg) |
| Barrel: | 3·75" (95mm) |
| Calibre: | 9mm |
| Rifling: | 6 groove, r/hand |
| Capacity: | Thirteen |
| Muz Vel: | 920 f/s (280 m/s) |
| Sights: | Fixed |

Italy
**BERETTA MODEL 92S**
Like the other Berettas seen here the Model 92S has a double-column magazine. This increases capacity but makes the arm rather bulky.

Italy
**BERETTA MODEL 84**
Note that the Model 84 is seen here with the magazine of the Model 81; the correct magazine is shown with the stripped arm (top left).

Italy
## BERETTA MODEL 81

As may be seen from comparison of the photographs, this pistol is virtually indistinguishable at a glance from the Model 84 shown on page 155 (below). This is not surprising, for a good many of the components are identical. The real difference between the two lies in their calibre: the Model 81 is designed to fire the 7·65mm cartridge, as opposed to the 9mm Short cartridge of the Model 84. The only components that differ between the two models are the barrel and the magazine spring and follower, which are necessarily narrower in the Model 81. The same basic magazine is used, but in the Model 81 its internal width is reduced as required by the two long grooves on either side; the magazine has been removed to show these. The weapon is operated in exactly the same way as the Model 84. Its external hammer, which is cocked by the action of the slide, may be lowered quite safely under the pressure of the thumb; thus, the weapon may be carried with a round in the chamber with no risk of accidental discharge. The magazine catch and safety are both reversible, for use by either hand. All these modern pistols are well made and finished, and their anodized aluminium frames make them light. They are reported as being very reliable mechanically, although double-column magazines make them rather bulky. This, of course, is the price which has to be paid for their unusually large magazine capacity. Along with the Beretta Model 84 and Model 92S, both of which are also illustrated on the colour spread, the Model 81 went into full-scale production in 1976. The Italian Army still retains some 9mm Beretta Model 1934 pistols (see pages 134-136), but the standard pistol of the Italian services (also in service with Egypt, Israel and the Nigerian police) is currently the 9mm Beretta Model 1951, a locked-breech pistol—the first Beretta of its kind—which went into full-scale production in 1957.

*The side view of the Beretta Model 81's magazine shows the double-column arrangement of the 7·65mm rounds. This gives a capacity of 12 rounds, but makes the butt rather bulky.*

Italy
## BERETTA MODEL 92S

This is the latest Beretta pistol in production at the time of writing (1980) and first appeared in 1976. It is an improved version of the Model 92, which was the 1951 model; this was taken into service by various armies and was also sold commercially under the trade name of "Brigádier", having first been made in quantity in 1957. Like the Model 1951 (currently the standard pistol of the Italian armed forces) the Models 92 and 92S fire the 9mm Parabellum round; the 92S is thus larger and more powerful than the Models 81 (7·65mm) and 84 (9mm Short) seen with it on the colour spread. Models 81 and 84 are blowback arms but, because of the powerful cartridge used, the Model 1951 was a locked-breech arm—the first Beretta of this type—and so are the Models 92 and 92S. The Model 92S is loaded in the orthodox way by the insertion of a 13-round box magazine into the butt and the manual operation of the slide, which cocks the hammer and chambers a round. Pressure of the fired case drives back the barrel and slide, which are locked by a block. After travelling about ·3in (8mm), the locking block is pivoted downward and disengages from the slide. The barrel then stops, but the slide continues to the rear to complete the reloading cycle. The chief difference between the Model 92S and its predecessor, the Model 92, is that the safety catch of the 92S is on the slide instead of on the frame. It has a double-column magazine, which increases capacity but makes the pistol's butt rather bulky.

Italy
## BERETTA MODEL 84

This pistol and the Model 81 described on the facing page are very similar: the two captions should be read in conjunction. A good deal has been written about the famous Beretta company earlier in this book (notably on page 136) and need not be repeated here. In 1976, Beretta put the Model 81 and Model 84 pistols into production, together with a more powerful Model 92; all of them share certain characteristics. Unlike the more powerful Model 92, however, the Model 84 is designed to fire the 9mm Short cartridge. As this is a relatively low-powered round, the weapon works on simple blowback, without any requirement for a breech-locking system. Manual retraction of the slide cocks the hammer and chambers a round on its forward motion. The recoil of the fired case thrusts the slide backward, compressing the recoil spring as it does so, and allows the firing cycle to continue. When the slide is forward and the pistol ready to fire, the extractor protrudes slightly from the slide, thus constituting a visual and manual indication of the pistol's state of readiness. There is also a manual safety which is operable either left- or right-handed. The pistol has a double-column magazine which makes the butt rather large. It is regretted that, when this pistol was photographed, the magazine belonging to the Model 81—with its two long grooves—was inadvertently substituted for the magazine of the Model 84. The correct magazine—no long grooves; holding thirteen 9mm rounds—is shown with the stripped Model 84 on the colour spread.

# Picture Credits

Unless otherwise credited, all pictures in this book were taken by Bruce Scott in the Weapons Museum, School of Infantry, Warminster, Wiltshire; or in the Pattern Room, Royal Small Arms Factory, Enfield Lock (pages 68-69; 106-107; 142-143).

The publisher wishes to thank the following organizations and invidivuals who have supplied photographs for this book. Photographs have been credited by page number; where more than one photograph appears on a page, references are made in the order of the columns across the page and then from top to bottom. The following abbreviations have been used: BBC: BBC Hulton Picture Library; IWM: Imperial War Museum, London; MARS: Military Archive &Research Service, London; NAM: National Army Museum, London; PNWA: Peter Newark's Western Americana.

8: Federal Bureau of Investigation; 8-9: NAM; 10: NAM/PNWA/IWM; 11: US Army; 12-13: NAM/BBC/US Army; 14: NAM/IWM; 15: US Army; 23: NAM; 30: Library of Congress; 35: NAM; 42: Musee de l'Armee, Paris; 59: NAM; 74: NAM; 78: MARS; 87: BBC; 91: IWM; 92: IWM; 92-93: US Army; 94: BBC; 95: IWM/NAM; 96: IWM/US Army; 97: NAM; US Army; 101: NAM; 104: NAM; 105: BBC; 112: IWM; 124-125: US Army (2); 128: Novosti; 132-133: MARS/IWM (2); 136: NAM; 137: US Army; 145: Institute of Military Science, Helsinki (MARS); 148: IWM; 152: IWM: 156: Beretta SPA, Brescia (MARS).

# Bibliography


| Title | Author/Editor | Place and year of publication | |
|---|---|---|---|
| Cartridges of the World | Barnes | Chicago | 1969 |
| British Military Firearms | Blackmore | London | 1961 |
| Pistols of the World | Blair | London | 1968 |
| United States Firearms | Butler | New York | 1971 |
| Adams Revolvers | Chamberlain and Taylerson | London | 1976 |
| Manual of Firearms | Deane | London | 1858 |
| Georgian Pistols | Dixon | London | 1971 |
| The Revolver | Dove | London | 1858 |
| The Webley Story | Dowell | Leeds | 1962 |
| English Pistols and Revolvers | George | London | 1961 |
| The Gun | Greener | London | 1881 |
| Remington Historical Treasury of American Guns | Grossett and Dunlap | New York | 1966 |
| A History of the Colt Revolver | Haven and Belden | New York | 1960 |
| German Pistols and Revolvers | Hogg | London | 1971 |
| Illustrated Encyclopedia of Firearms | Hogg | London | 1978 |
| Pistols of the World | Hogg and Weeks | London | 1978 |
| Treatise on Military Small Arms and Ammunition | HMSO | London | 1888 |
| Textbook of Small Arms | HMSO | London | 1909 |
| Textbook for Small Arms | HMSO | London | 1929 |
| History of Smith and Wesson | Jinks | Los Angeles | 1977 |
| Japanese Infantry Weapons of World War Two | Markham | London | 1976 |
| Smith and Wesson 1867-1945 | Neal and Jinks | New York | 1966 |
| Encyclopedia of Firearms | Peterson | London | 1964 |
| The Book of the Pistol | Pollard | London | 1917 |
| Automatic Pistols | Pollard | London | 1920 |
| The British Soldier's Firearms | Roads | London | 1964 |
| Two Hundred Years of American Firearms | Serven | Northfield Ill | 1975 |
| Book of Pistols and Revolvers | Smith | Harrisburg Pa | 1977 |
| Small Arms of the World | Smith and Smith | London | 1973 |
| Pistols; a Modern Encyclopedia | Stebbins | Harrisburg Pa | 1961 |
| The Inglis Browning Hi-Power Pistol | Stevens | Ottawa | 1974 |
| The Revolver 1818-1865 | Taylerson, Andrews, Frith | London | 1968 |
| The Revolver 1865-1888 | Taylerson | London | 1966 |
| The Revolver 1889-1914 | Taylerson | London | 1970 |
| Revolving Arms | Taylerson | London | 1967 |
| Luger | Walter | London | 1977 |
| Jane's Infantry Weapons 1979-1980 | Weeks (Ed) | London | 1980 |
| The Illustrated Book of Pistols | Wilkinson | London | 1979 |
| Textbook of Automatic Pistols | Wilson/Hogg | London | 1975 |
| Automatic Pistol Shooting | Winans | London | 1915 |
| The Art of Revolver Shooting | Winans | London | 1901 |
| Early Percussion Firearms | Winant | London | 1970 |
| Firearms Curiosa | Winant | New York | 1970 |
| Standard Directory of Proof Marks | Wirnsberger | New Jersey | 1975 |

# GUIDES IN THIS SERIES............

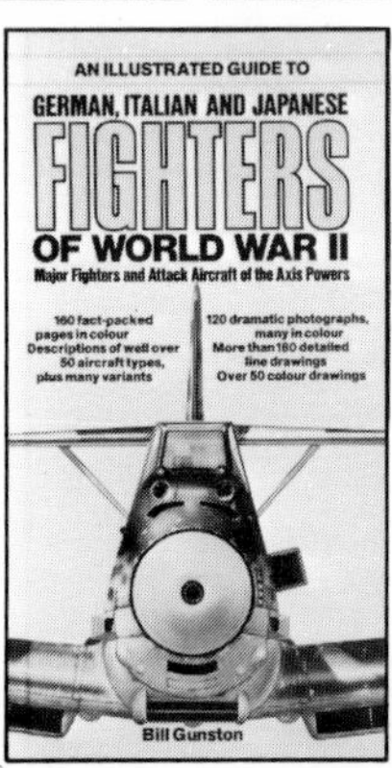

- ✻ Each has 160 fact-filled pages
- ✻ Each is colourfully illustrated with more than one hundred dramatic photographs, and often with superb technical drawings
- ✻ Each contains concisely presented data and accurate descriptions of major international weapons
- ✻ Each represents tremendous value

**Further titles in this series are in preparation**

**Your military library will be incomplete without them**

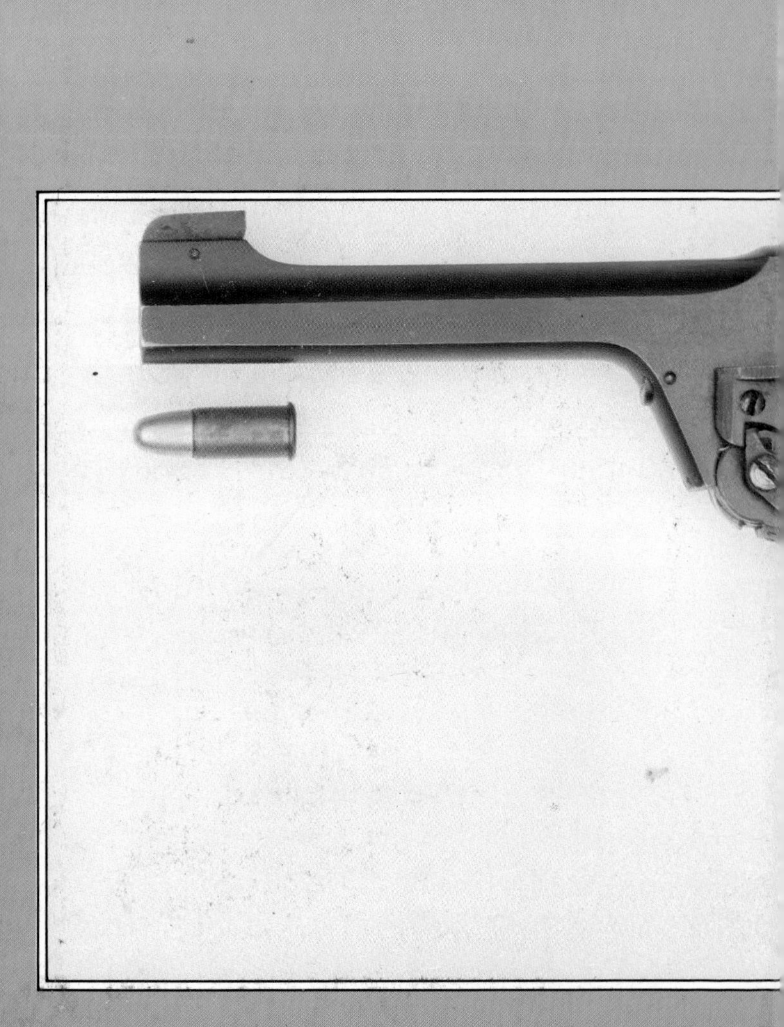